# THE
# EMOTIONALLY INTELLIGENT DENTAL OFFICE

by
Dr. Steven Hymovitch

ISBN: 978-1-7327991-5-8 (soft cover)
ISBN: 978-1-7327991-6-5 (e-book)

Steven Hymovitch, DDS, MBA, CEC
Scottsdale Leadership and Coaching Center
8121 E. Indian Bend Road, Suite 128
Scottsdale, AZ 85250

Final Prepress and Production: Parisian Phoenix Publishing
*Cover art elements LightFieldStudios/istockphoto.com, freepik.com, vecteezy.com, rawpixels.com*

Printed in the United States of America

# DEDICATION

My path to pursue success in life and my profession was inspired early on by my parents. Day after day, I watched them treat people with respect and truly care about the perspectives of others. Rather than jumping to conclusions, they listened and really wanted to know how other people think.

My parents led with empathy and genuine interest in the varying viewpoints of family, friends, neighbors, and business associates, long before emotional intelligence became so well studied by scholars and business leaders. I'm so grateful for the example and wisdom they showed me.

Inspired by the early examples and teachings of my parents, my wife, Julie, and our five children continue to help me with the building blocks of my journey to utilize emotional intelligence in daily life. Developing healthy people skills is a lifelong journey for many of us, and my wife and children keep me in check as I seek to grow emotional intelligence skills in all parts of life.

Over the last three decades, I've been privileged to achieve success as an endodontist, practice leader, business owner and entrepreneur. While any journey has its ups and downs, my success is a result of the talented and dedicated teams in our practices. Emotional intelligence is just as important as the education, experience and technical skills sets we share with each other and our patients.

Our doctors, office managers, and patient care professionals help me to be better every day.

In turn, we strive to share these "soft" skills with referring dental offices and other business partners.

Thank you to the team members that inspire me!

# CONTENTS

*"Dr. Hymovitch strategically describes the importance of E.I. and positions it in a way that is useful for all. This book is a guideline to awareness of all emotions; it thoroughly explains how to navigate through the complexities of all scenarios while providing the tools to do so."*

~ DR ROBERT W. PASSLOFF, ENDODONTIST, DMD, President,
Advanced Root Canal Specialists of Massachusetts

*This book will be a road-map for every leader and healthcare provider aspiring for personal and practice growth. Understanding and practicing Emotional Intelligence will significantly impact your practice and your life! This is a must read!!!!*

~ DEE FISCHER, Founder, Fischer Professional Group, helping doctors create systems, accountability, and passion in the workplace.
Awarded 2023 Women in DSO Leadership for Business Excellence

*This book by Dr. Hymovitch will make you see yourself and others through individual life experiences so conflict and social interactions can be both understood and resolved. This applies to the dental office setting as well as in personal life. The introduction to self-well-being is just the start.*

~ DR. LIVINGSTON CHEN, 30-year practice owner,
Promenade Dental, Toronto, Canada

*This book on Emotional Intelligence is a must have for anyone wanting to have their dental staff work cohesively and with the common goal of a great work environment. The benefits we have seen extend beyond work, your patients and all staff but improved our personal relationships too. This practical guidance to Emotional Intelligence has provided me with an awareness and understanding to work towards positive outcomes that has improved my relationship with my dental staff and in turn their mutual relationships to each other. We had a good office environment before... now we have a better one! Thanks Dr H.!*

~ DR. MICHAEL SILVER BSC. DDS. M.S., Premier Dentistry,
West Palm Beach, Florida

*"The Emotionally Intelligent Dental Office is a must read for anyone looking to take their practice to the next level and significantly improve their leadership skills. Study this book carefully, it's endless amount of information and useful tips are extraordinarily helpful for healthcare professionals, including those outside of dentistry."*

~DR. NATHAN LAUFER, MD, CM, FACC, FCCP, FACP, FRCP (C)
Founder and Medical Director of the
Heart and Vascular Center of Arizona

*Like Steve Hymovitch...the Endodontist, Business Owner and Author of this book...I know a thing or two about running a successful dental practice, including expanding services to implant, restorations and cosmetic dentistry in a no-insurance practice. And like Steve, I believe applying Emotional Intelligence is so very important to keeping my practice healthy, as I feel E.I. is as important in all aspects of our lives. I'd agree with Steve when he writes that for him, E.I. is so much more important than I.Q. While I know it is currently one of those 'buzz word' phrases, if we all learned to apply a little more E.I. into our lives, and even though this book is titled, The Emotionally Intelligent Dental Office, you really don't have to be a Dentist to enjoy it and get lots from it.*

*I feel this book is unique (and a darn good read), as much because it is aimed at Dentists looking to create a more harmonious practice (and personal life) as it's written from Steve's often self-deprecating POV, with lots of heartfelt insights and good big globs of humor. I think you will have a great time reading, learning, and laughing along at the Emotionally Intelligent Dental Office. Now, let's all go out and spread some good E.I., our practices, our lives; the world surely needs it.*

~ DR. MITCHEL JOSEPHS, DDS, Radio Host of "Tooth Talk," live call-in show on dental health, Palm Beach, Florida. Dr. Josephs is on staff at JFK Medical Center and is a Faculty Advisory Board member at McGill University's Faculty of Dentistry and serves on the Medical Board of *U.S. News and World Report*

# PREFACE

*When dealing with people, remember you are not dealing with creatures of logic, but with creatures of emotion.*
~ DALE CARNEGIE

The late and great Dale Carnegie spent a lifetime teaching us how to win friends and influence people to achieve rewarding and successful relationships. One thing I've learned during three decades of building thriving dental, endodontic and oral surgery medical practices is that people make our offices work whether servicing patients or keeping the back office running smoothly.

All the smarts and hard work in the world can only take us so far in our professional or personal lives. How many times have you conveyed the most logical argument that is sure to win over a skeptical colleague and it gets blown to bits with an emotional response that seemingly comes from left field? You scratch your head in disbelief and double down with more facts and substance to prove your point of view but a successful outcome seems elusive.

Often times, the emotional response can override the intellectual or thinking brain no matter how reasonable. Behavioral scientists and scholars suggest that emotional intelligence is just as important as I.Q. in developing successful relationships and outcomes at work and in life.

No matter what the experience, we can choose how we want to respond and to encourage a positive outcomes that benefit both sides of the relationship and our patients. Investing a little time to develop these "soft skills" in all of us is worth the time and effort and will pay daily dividends.

Please join me on this journey in reading *The Emotionally Intelligent Dental Office*. You'll find tons of down-to-Earth examples that hit home mixed with plain talk, useful tools and advice to grow and enhance your emotional intelligence on the work front and in personal relationships. Wishing you a life filled with healthy relationships!

~ Dr. Steven Hymovich, DDS, MBA, CEC

# SECTION ONE
# The Basics of Emotional Intelligence

# INTRODUCTION
## Emotional Intelligence: What It Is, Why We Need It, and How We Get It

*"The secret to many a man's success in the world resides in his insight into the moods of men and his tact in dealing with them."*
~ J.G. HOLLAND

*"Be the person your dog thinks you are!"*
~ J.W. STEPHENS

*"The most important thing in life is to always be yourself. Unless you can be Batman, in which case, always be Batman."*
~ UNKNOWN

Welcome to my second book, *The Emotionally Intelligent Dental Office*. If you read the first, *The Dentist Who Gets It*, you know I am the all-knowing best boss, most world-renowned endodontist, and best executive/life coach on the planet. If not, take it from me: I am all these things and more.

Actually...the reason I mention the first book, beyond trying to get you to seek it out, is that in the middle of it I expound on the concept of emotional intelligence (EI) and how it is so essential, not only in the work environment (especially the dental office), but also in one's personal life. The chapter written on EI was only a smidgen of the first book, but while writing it, I realized the necessity for an entire book on the subject.

A quick spin around any local Barnes & Noble will reveal that I wasn't the only person with this bright idea. You know how it is: a new catch-phrase or cause catches fire, somebody starts vlogging about this or that, maybe Doctor Phil centers one of his shows around it, and all of a sudden, the thing becomes really popular or trending. So, it seems with the current popularity around emotional intelligence.

The first thing that separates this book from any other on the topic of EI is that it is written by me, and I will directly relate EI to a dental practice.

Secondly, I will strive to present this material in an entertaining manner. Being formally trained in, and having read lots of those other EI books, I know how much more fun it is to learn something that sets a light tone—something that might make you giggle at times and that makes you feel like the author is more your friend than a psychologist coming down to your level for a day.

Besides, I'm not a psychologist. I don't even play one on T.V.

## What is EI and How Do You Get It?

Emotional intelligence is a human being's ability to recognize and understand his or her emotions, as well as the ability to acknowledge the same in others. Once you get a handle on EI, you will not only be able to understand the emotions of your friends, family, and co-workers, but you will also be able to influence the emotions of others. When I refer to influencing though, I am not talking about manipulation. We have all met those folks who use their awareness like an evil superpower, riding roughshod over co-workers, families, lovers, and siblings in classic passive-aggressive measures. Don't worry, I have this kind of power-play covered as you will learn how to recognize when others attempt to use their own emotional awareness to employ passive-aggressive tactics.

What I mean by influence in regard to other people's emotions is a better understanding of somebody else's mood and, how, through your words or actions, you can alleviate their bad day or a hiccup moment or even add to some good feelings they might be having.

See? Nothing untoward here. The more you lock in your emotional intelligence, the more you will come to understand that only positive uses—even if you are in the middle of criticizing someone—pay dividends.

When I refer to emotional intelligence as a person's ability to recognize and understand his or her emotions, I don't intend for you to go forth into the raging of the light stoic and unfeeling. Growing EI is not about controlling normal, healthy, and necessary human emotions. It's about becoming aware of them. Life is about friction—for our purposes here, the friction of personalities coming to work together. We all know damn well that everybody has got baggage on the carousel of life. To my way of thinking, the conflicts of life—and most of the fun—come when our bag bumps into someone else's bag. That's the key here, and why EI is so important, especially in a work environment.

Friction, tension, conflict, push-and-pull—whatever you want to call it—is bound to happen when humans interact. Without problems occurring from time to time in our lives, we'd all be game show hosts, and who wants that kind of a boring existence?

What's important to the daily drama of bumping into one another is how to keep things moving forward, how to work to positive outcomes, and in the end, trying to get along, especially at work. It's listening to a co-worker's recent personal challenge or knowing that they are going through one, lending an encouraging word or well-placed smile, and consciously avoiding bothering them further.

Sounds pretty good, right?

Ask yourself these questions:

𝔀 "Why wouldn't I want to be a more effective and happier worker?"

𝔀 "Why wouldn't I want to learn how to get the very best from my employees, my employer, or even from patients?"

Emotional intelligence employed in the workplace, in our case, the dental office, will make all of our jobs easier and create a happier and more productive work environment. And even more, the better our EI, the better it will make our life outside of the office.

How? Well, ya gotta read the book. This is just the intro.

Building your emotional intelligence muscles is not hard, but it does take a bit of time and attention. As you would suspect, when considering human emotions, trying to wrestle yourself to an awareness of them—be it our own or someone else's—requires executing some deep dives. We must put aside some well-worn prejudices, and perhaps face some stuff we don't encounter often. To be sure, in this wacky, disconnected-connected world we live in, by sullying forth to grow and use your EI, you'll be bucking the latest trend. You'll be prone to talk to and interact with people more. You will be better focused on things in front of you in real time that demand your attention, things that can't be managed just with a tweet or text.

But, as I said at the beginning, Doctor H. (yes, me) is along every step of the way. I promise we're going to have a good time and learn a lot. At the end of the day, you are going to be an even better you, *all without changing you one smidgen.*

This last bit is so significant I want you to reread it: *all without changing you one smidgen.*

That's the thing with building awareness. While learning more about emotional intelligence, in bettering your life and the life of the folks around you, you do not have to start a journey that will twist you into psychological knots or that takes you away from who you are or what you believe. You don't even have to progress up a series of steps. The finer your EI gets, the easier life will get. As you already *have* EI, you're not changing to get it, just fine tuning yourself.

Dan Goleman, Ph.D., psychologist, *New York Times* bestselling author and arguably the father of modern emotional intelligence, says that EI has four parts: *self-awareness, managing emotion, managing empathy,* and lastly one that's so very important these days, *social skills.* I agree with the good doctor. We will do a deeper dive on all four of these parts, but for now, here's a brief overview.

## Self-Awareness

Self-awareness is about our capacity for introspection, for understanding our own feelings, motives, and triggers, as well as understanding how we are separate from others. Growing a healthy emotional intelligence and recognizing this selflessness will help us develop a less-conceited view. As we grow our self-awareness, we realize that there are other people—other selfs—out there with their own feelings, motives, and triggers to be considered and respected.

## Managing Emotion

*Managing emotion* is our ability to be open to feeling our feelings to put them in perspective, or modulate them in a sense. Once we can do this, we can look to understanding the emotions in others.

## Managing Empathy

Managing empathy is being able to find and act on perspective when we come to walk in somebody else's shoes. Dr. Goleman calls this our ability to read other people, to go beyond feeling for somebody else, and to put our sharing of similar feelings into play. Empathy has three types: cognitive, personal, and empathetic.

Psychologist Mark Davis weighs in specifically on these three types of empathy. He refers to *cognitive empathy* as "perspective taking." Simply put, this is seeing things from another person's point of view and coming to understand where that person is coming from. Secondly, there is the deeper *personal distress*, how you suddenly become very frightened for that victim running from the slasher killer in the scary movie, or how you feel terrible when a friend is crying on your shoulder. Davis calls this process "emotional contagion" or being infected with another's emotions just because we have these emotions ourselves.

And the last one is how we tend to define empathy on a general basis or *empathic concern*. This is our ability to recognize another's emotional state, to feel in-tune with that state. If we determine that it is a negative or distressful emotion, we feel and show appropriate concern.

## Social Skills

*Social skills* are those traits that we use to communicate with other human beings. They can be verbal as well as non-verbal, and can be facilitated, both positively and negatively, by a whole host of means.

***

See, there is a lot to this stuff.

I mentioned the fun aspect of this book. Don't fret, it's in here. What follows is not all loaded up with psychologist's opinions.

Yes, guys like Goleman and Davis and plenty more men and women who weigh in on emotional intelligence have worthy points to make, and I am all for reading what they have written. But none of what I wrote here would be worth anything if I didn't give you real examples from my experience, personal and professional.

This is where the fun is in this book: I show how wonderfully I come to use my evolved EI and how I completely screw the pooch on many occasions! Like you, and every other human on the planet, I make mistakes, and need to constantly keep working at this stuff.

Awareness is the key here, and we need to be aware, right from the outset, that we are flawed. Often our intellect and emotion work against one another. You, me, your kids, spouse, co-worker, golf buddy—and indeed your dentist and his or her staff—are all works in progress.

With emotional intelligence you can flip the script on a lot of the negative. You can give that emotional stuff I mentioned less weight in your life and in the lives of others. You will come to view conflict as opportunity, react more fluidly on-the-fly, listen better, and cultivate empathy to a razor's edge, both in the office and beyond it. As I always say, and will point out again and again, cultivating EI will pay dividends across all the relationships in your life.

This is about self-awareness that you can use to become aware of others. Getting to the the root of emotional intelligence gives you power, an edge. It can calm you. It will allow you to see to your tasks more clearly. It will bring you to an understanding of your strengths and weaknesses. And it will also keep you from unduly lashing out.

You might come to see ingrained habits or prejudices you have held onto for no reason or for too long. You may come to see that which consistently prompts you to create unrealistic expectations for others or yourself. In the end, you might even be able to help someone whether they are encountering a crisis or are just in a bad mood. This is just the tip of the iceberg of what self-awareness and emotional intelligence can do.

Remember the advice dearly-departed Patrick Swayze as John Dalton gives his bouncer crew in the movie *Roadhouse*? He keeps repeating to these rough-and-tumble guys that the first order of bouncing someone from the bar is to "be nice."

Swayze's advice is reiterated in real life by billionaire business owner and celebrity Mark Cuban (probably most recognizable for his role on *Shark Tank*). Cuban told *Vanity Fair* magazine that one of the simplest skills to succeeding in business is to be nice. Referring to his own early career when all Cuban wanted was to make the deal and jump from each success to another, Cuban claims he was so unpleasant that he wouldn't have done business with himself. These days he finds nice rules out: "Nice sells," he is quoted as saying.

I guarantee there will come plenty of times in the book where you'll stop and say, "Really, Dr. H.? Um, this is kind of obvious, no?"

Sure, lots of this stuff is just about being nice, thoughtful, polite, and empathetic. It's standard stuff that we have all been taught. Emotional intelligence is not rocket science. (And really, is anything but rocket science rocket science?) We have it in us. Usually, yes *usually*, we want to act this way anyway.

What I will do in this book is nudge you in the right direction, prompt you from your lethargy (or extract your nose from your cell phone screen), and help you recognize the behaviors that we all share that compromise a healthy state of mind and sound awareness. Given the way our brains work, we really are primed and set for emotional intelligence. We just need to have our browser reset every now and again, sit back and take a breath, maybe shift our priorities a bit in this wacky world we live in, and connect to that which is essential.

In the end, I truly believe, and I would not have written this book without this belief, that *emotional intelligence trumps I.Q.* Working in the sciences as I have for many years, I've encountered plenty of so-called geniuses—men and women who spoke, acted, and worked on a level that I could never reach. But rarely, if ever, have I understood any of them, nor did I want to. Good for their big brain, I say, but I'll trade smarts for caring any day.

The guy or gal who has a handle, even slightly, on who they are and what makes them tick, who understands the importance of trying to be slightly more emotionally intelligent every day, is the person I want in my foxhole. So, come with me. I promise a wild, informative, bumpy ride ahead into the wonders of emotional intelligence.

Without further ado, let me make you aware in Chapter 1.

# **1** Our Brain

That which makes us human—the very nature of our bodies and brains, as well as sociability and habits—makes it possible for us to cultivate the highest form of emotional intelligence on the planet. But this very same stuff, the very "meat and taters" of who we are, also keeps us from growing our emotional intelligence. The following are some of the things that get in our way and what we can do about them.

## Hey Neighbor: The Sections of Your Brain

I remember an original *Star Trek* episode where an alien disguised as a very attractive lady invades the Enterprise and steals Mr. Spock's brain ("Spock's Brain," season three premier). Yeah, I know, this was 1960s sci-fi—but just stay with me.

When Captain Kirk confronts the alien invader and orders her to put Spock's brain back to its rightful place in his pointy-eared head, it was brought to light that her initial intelligence was only temporary. Not understanding Kirk's demands, she cries out in frustration that she doesn't know how she took the Vulcan's brain in the first place while Dr. McCoy explains that her mind is functioning on a very simple level due to mental atrophy caused by non-use. It's ironic that the very organ that aids and abets our emotional intelligence, our brain, may betray us when we try to cultivate E.I.

Our little-engine-that-can gets in the way of our emotions, with our cognitive skills often clogging the wheels of our instinct, memory, and judgment. The innate abilities we have that help us formulate opinions often keep us locked in them. Everyone has this daily whammy-jammy going on in their noggin.

## PART ONE: **Basal Ganglia**

There are three parts to our brain function. The *basal ganglia*, often referred to as the reptilian part of our brain, is the oldest of the three if we look at general evolution. The basal ganglia controls vital functions like heart rate, breathing, and our need for procreation. It's responsible for our survival and prompts us to the classic "fight or flight" response. It allows us to regard the world around us in symbols and shapes. This brain region is the cause of your gut reaction, and also controls your inhibitions at the most basic level, which can lead to reactionary, sometimes compulsive behavior. Most of what is in the basal ganglia exists on an unconscious level and is generally inaccessible, but it's there.

Stress is the kryptonite of the reptilian brain. It will keep us stuck to the point where we will not even use, or will ignore, the next two higher levels of our brain. But Stress can be countered by our most basic human need, *breathing*. You know how it usually goes when someone attacks your personal space: the hairs on the back of your neck rise and your heart rate increases. If you can calm yourself, breathe, count to ten, or even meditate, your stress level will almost always decrease.

## PART TWO: **The Limbic System**

The *limbic system* is the brain as it first appeared in mammals. Aren't you happy you are one? It is more mature on the evolutionary scale than our reptilian brain and serves as the seat of our most profound emotions. The limbic system is our emotional center. It stores our value judgments and the memories of behaviors that produce positive and negative experiences. The information here is mostly subconscious, existing below our awareness.

I am sure you can easily understand the good and bad of the limbic system regarding emotional intelligence. This is the place in our noggin where assumptions and prejudices form. While decisions made without emotional considerations could be fatal, decisions made only with them, using just this part of our brains, are not a good idea either. Not being able to control those emotions or at least understand them can lead to some leaky EI.

## PART THREE: **Neocortex**

Lastly, there is the *neocortex*, really big with us humans—best not leave home without it. This is where we manage abstract thought, negotiate, develop and learn languages, and the place where our imagination lies. The neocortex is your thinking and learning center. Here we reason through emotions, battle prejudices, add more information to our worldview, and build on our empathy. This vast section of the brain (taking up 76% of your gray matter) is also the root of our ability for social interaction.

The neocortex is also the place where connections are made, between what Yale neuroscientists call the neighborhoods of your brain[1]. If this section is injured, a human could lose speech, space recognition, eyesight, and the ability to recognize social cues.

We need all of these sections—*the basal ganglia, the limbic system and the neocortex*—for our wonderful little organ to function at its fullest. When you consider that we supposedly use only ten percent of what we have up there, it's amazing what we are able to accomplish. The thing is, these three parts of the brain do not operate independently. Those neighborhoods intertwine with one another, working synergistically, interconnecting through myriad sparks and pathways. They are kind of like neighbors meeting for early summer evening chats while leaning on fences and porches.

A lot is going on up there, but within all of these levels, rest assured, we can often be led astray from emotional intelligence.

## EI is Good for Your Brain

There exists a chasm of difference between knowing about something and putting that something into practice, even when we desire to put that knowledge into action. One part of the brain deals with the knowing (the neocortex) and another the doing (the limbic). To change habits and alter thinking and behavior, we need to marry idea with action. Not only is this marriage crucial in developing our emotional intelligence, but it also makes our brains stronger.

When growing emotional intelligence, we unknowingly make changes between the rational and emotional pathways of our brain or expand these pathways in new ways. Exercises such as slowing and considering our reactions, intellectually working to alleviate stress, finding a different perspective to stimuli, and building and implementing a broader sense of empathy cause an actual physical change to the brain.

Like the branches of a willow tree reaching and swaying in the breeze, the pathways of our brains reach out to other cells, creating thousands upon thousands of new connections across those brain neighborhoods (there's those friendly neighbors again). The neuroplasticity of our brains allows for seemingly endless changes, and the physical and functional properties continually evolve as our emotional intelligence grows.

We act on learned behavioral responses and past assumptions. We gravitate towards groupthink, hoping to be accepted, often blindly marching from safety out of sheer stubbornness. In effect, we are led by that wonderful

---

[1] Nenad Sestan, professor of neurobiology at Yale's Kavli Institute for Neuroscience, says the human brain is like a neighborhood which is better defined by the community living within its borders than its buildings.

"The neighborhoods get built quickly and then everything slows down and the neocortex focuses solely on developing connections, almost like an electrical grid," said Sestan. "Later when these regions are synchronized, the neighborhoods begin to take on distinct functional identities like Little Italy or Chinatown."

(https://news.yale.edu/2013/12/26/human-brain-development-symphony-three-movements; also Neuron, December 2013 issue)

thinking machine between our ears. We are drawn to fabulousness in the same measure as we are to folly, to good sense, and to bad.

Welcome to the contradiction that is the human being. The fact is, if you want to grow your emotional intelligence to the abilities and constraints your brain allows, you'll need to work hard to increase your awareness of these contradictions. By putting yourself through some training, and being mindful in new ways, you will not only beat back the ways your brain biologically impedes EI, but you can also grow your brain to new heights.

# 2 Psychological Enemy #1: Inertia

Now that we've discussed what the brain can do to improve emotional intelligence, let's talk specifically about how the brain can hamper our EI growth. What we battle most is *psychological inertia*, a fancy term that describes how we get stuck, spin our wheels over assumptions, or become waylaid under obstacles we create for ourselves.

Psychological inertia causes impediments in our actions and allows for the breakdown between data and interpretation. This spins the perceptions around concepts that we have been influenced by into prejudices that we may not even know exist. None of this is good for building EI or growing this big brain of ours.

At the end of this spectrum are not only the long-term habits we cultivate, but also the long-term abuses we allow. There are many reasons a person will stay in an abusive or unproductive relationship. Extricating oneself from these situations can be extremely difficult because of psychological-inertia quicksand. With more awareness comes more of the possibility of getting free.

We all have basic physical needs, just as we do psychological ones, although we are not always aware of the latter. Still, we attempt to satiate these needs time and again, even if what we do stunts our emotional intelligence and awareness. Often the comfort of the habit, even if we are aware of probable negative outcome, is enough to keep going us back to it. The devil we know is easier to deal with than the devil we don't.

Change is essential for growth, but it is also human nature to fight it. We fear the unknown so much that we avoid it, and more often than not, we get into what psychologist Albert Ellis called *awfulizing*[2]. He used the term to describe rationalizing the worst possible scenario—and refusing to make changes, in the now, to avoid it.

---

2 https://albertellis.org/2015/07/awfulizing-time/

## Lions and Tigers and Schema, Oh My!

In growing our awareness and our overall cognitive skills, we come to what psychologist Jean Piaget called *schemas* of cognitive development[3]. Simply put, schemas are mental structures that we create as we learn about the world.

While very young, if children are taught that the creature they play with at an aunt's house with four legs, fur, and a tongue that laps water from a bowl is called a dog, then, until they know better, they might think a cat or a rabbit is a dog. Until contradictory information enters into their experience, the schema (or basic mental framework) a child develops will not change.

This is a benign childhood example to be sure, so let's take the idea of the schema into adulthood. If the only female boss someone ever worked for was a difficult person, that employee might—even as an adult who knows better and has access to lots of information—form a schema to be wary female employers.

Even though logically it behooves people to judge each person, man or woman, on an individual basis, the bright light of logic doesn't often shine upon a schema. Regardless of how kind and knowledgeable the new boss might be, someone with a schema that connects "female," "boss" and "difficult person" might never change their preconceptions.

In children, schemas are usually less cemented and therefore more easily broken apart and challenged. But, depending on how deeply that schema has formed, adults will often build a wall of alternative reasons why reality does not hold to past perceptions. In many instances, people would rather keep their schema healthy and in place than face facts that challenge it—and, really, tell me you don't know this to be true...

People will also fashion responses and logical strategies to use for the slightest provocation, using language that is almost always negative. I like to refer to this as "the same old script." More than just set prejudices or modes of thinking, these responses are born from schemas. Schema set? If yes—cue the script and shut down the play even before the curtain rises!

We all see how triggers form. It's not hard. We can all too easily be set off by what we expect, or what we have seen played out before. In many cases, we become satiated from dysfunctional thinking that reaffirms our own schema. Our schema, our reality, brings us comfort and security. It's a wonder we ever get out of our own way.

## Habits

Habits, like schema, are a hard to break. Habits waylay our awareness and the further good construction of emotional intelligence. In the end though, if you can break a longstanding bad habit, you might find EI the very best new habit you could ever hope to have.

Dr. Maxwell Maltz, a plastic surgeon working in the 1950s, noticed that no matter what he did to a patient's face, it took three weeks for them to get used

---

3 https://www.simplypsychology.org/piaget.html

to the change. He considered this three-week rule as the basis to the theory that no matter what the situation might be, it takes humans three weeks to kill an old habit and form a new one.[4]

In 1960, Maltz published *Psycho-Cybernetics*[5], his book about this phenomenon and other theories he had formulated about his observations. Psycho-Cybernetics went on to sell more than 30 million copies. One could say that the good doctor's theories about habits became quite habit-forming themselves.

But folks enlisting Maltz's ideas came to repeat his minimum of about 21 days as gospel, not as the nebulous calculation the good doctor intended. The well-intentioned theorists and psychologists who followed Maltz got in the habit (sorry, I just can't help myself when the puns come this quickly) of claiming, as fact, that it takes 21 days to form a new habit. And that's how that common myth began.

So how long does it take to build a new habit? How long does it take to alter a smidgen of your thoughts to new action? How long will it take from the time you read this so-informative book until you are enlightened? Modern studies of habits lean towards the assumption that it takes two months to form new habits and thoughts[6]. Considering emotional intelligence, how long it takes for it to become habit forming, depends on *you*.

The point here is that it takes time to alter your actions and thinking. You shouldn't rush it. Remember, you're building new brain cheese, probably jumping past some schemas, throwing open the door on some long-ago locked rooms in your head and heart. This takes time!

---

4 https://science.howstuffworks.com/life/inside-the-mind/human-brain/form-a-habit.htm (But remember, these are just theories.)
5 https://www.psycho-cybernetics.com/about/
6 https://www.ncbi.nlm.nih.gov/pmc/articles/PMC3505409/
https://www.ncbi.nlm.nih.gov/pmc/articles/PMC3505409/ (*British Journal of General Practice*, December 2012.)

# 3 Psychological Enemy #2: Triangulation

Lest we think the interaction between two people stays between two people, let's consider the concept of triangulation. It can happen in a home, on a boat, in the rain or on a train, (if you happen to be in a Seussian frame of mind). For my purposes, and quite frankly, where I see it happen all the time, is in the office.

Think of that old game of "Telephone" or "Whisper Down the Alley": one person tells one person, and that person tells another. But unlike Telephone where words get jumbled and or replaced by others, in triangulation, the essence of two people interacting gets told to a third, with negative impact.

ᕙ "Can you believe what he/she said to me?"

ᕙ "What am I supposed to make of that?"

ᕙ "See, how he/she acts?"

This usually causes the last person participating, the third leg of the triangle, to come to a frequently negative conclusion and form an opinion influenced by the speaker in the middle of the chain. As humans build relationships, it is natural to "dish" or at the very least, talk with and sometimes inadvertently but often intentionally, about our colleagues, but the problem escalates when adding or talking about a third person. The middle man is the problem here.

Triangulation magnifies a conflict and spreads bad juju, as rarely is there a solution floated in the mix. Suddenly the personalities in the office are playing against one another like a bad episode of *Survivor*, where it's anyone's guess who will get voted off the island—and if you are the boss or owner, this becomes your problem and a reflection of your office culture. This wastes valuable time, and further triangulation can reinforce a conflict, as gossip usually gets back to the person who is the subject of the gossip. This, of course, can erode office relationships and cause additional risks.

## The Karpman Drama Triangle

The last thing I want to throw at you is a lot of psychological jargon, but there is a lot of science behind emotional intelligence. Tons of theory and thought has gone into explaining why we do the things we do and how better to do what we do with one another. As a rule, I tend towards not taking every morsel a scientist or a talking head says as the gospel truth. I believe first and foremost in what I have seen occur in thirty years of running my dental practices. One big-head psychological theory that I do believe though concerns triangulation. It is the *Karpman Drama Triangle*. [7]

Stephen Karpman was a student of Eric Berne, the father of transactional analysis[8]. *Transactional analysis* is the modern psychological study of people's relations and interactions. Karpman's Drama Triangle takes a deeper dive into the types of interactions one encounters and the roles they play in triangulation.

**Victim:** First and foremost, there is the *victim*. It's pretty apparent that there can be no chance at a nice juicy triangulation without one person feeling that they have been slighted. This is the guy or gal who complains about some wrong done to them.

"Can you believe what she/he just said to me?"

As we all know, there are eternal victims who always think they're being slighted somehow. These are people who see the world as conspiring against them. They serve as the leg that supports a drama triangle.

**Rescuer:** Secondly, there is the *rescuer*, the person the victim goes to or who reaches out to the victim. Most people have, at one time, found themselves in the rescuer's role or something close to it. Just as it is human nature to gossip, it is also human nature to want to help. But helping the victim in a potential triangulation scenario means that the rescuer is *enabling*.

There are folks who sometimes play the nurturer/the eternal rescuer and who pride themselves on being heroes. Without a victim, the rescuer has no one to pick up and dust off. The rescuer is just as looming a presence as the victim, waiting for a chance to show the world how wonderful they are.

**Persecutor/Villain:** The third person in Karpman's triangle is the *persecutor* or *villain*. Depending on the victim's perception, the villain may or may not be entirely responsible for an attack or slight. But, in most cases the villain does something—be it a full-on critique or a trivial unknowing aside—that prods and pricks at the victim in some way. To be sure, as with the victim and the rescuer, there are those people who play the villain role to a hilt.

In triangulation, victim, villain, and rescuer roles can morph, ebb, and flow with any person taking on one role or another, although those who define themselves in these roles usually stick to them. In other words, if the role of victim, villain or rescuer becomes a core part of a person's identity and how they see themselves, they will intentionally exploit opportunities to reinforce that role.

7 https://karpmandramatriangle.com/
8 https://ericberne.com/transactional-analysis/

Luckily, Karpman believed that humans are capable of infinite personal growth and positive interactions. What leads to infinite personal growth and positive interactions leads to emotional intelligence. Karpman believed there are several steps we can take to avoid triangulation.

## Avoiding Triangulation

**Avoid being recruited.** You might have to act like Switzerland in the office and stay neutral to somebody else's conflict. Literally, throw up your hands with an "I don't want to hear about it" gesture and attitude. Do not be the rescuer or the listener.

You might also advise the two people to talk to a manager or boss, someone who can act as a mediator in these circumstances. In some cases though, bringing in a superior to help two parties resolve their conflict can escalate feelings of persecution, resulting in one person complaining that the other is throwing them under the proverbial bus.

As a boss, I have seen plenty of interoffice conflicts teetering on the edge of triangulation, conflicts that I am damn glad someone alerted me to, so that they could be dealt with and stopped before things got totally out of hand.

What are my tips?

The most important part of defusing conflict and battling against the possibility of triangulation is to air the problem quickly. One of the golden rules of good office relations, and something a good boss learns directly from emotional intelligence, is that direct and immediate interaction works best: it cuts the legs out of the triangle of triangulation. There is no possibility of getting others involved when it's only two people discussing the issue. If the two parties directly involved can't work it out, then the head of the office must act as an impartial mediator privately and expediently.

# 4 Psychological Enemy #3: Data vs. Interpretation

There can be a vast chasm of difference between the data we take in and our interpretation of it. Data vs. interpretation is a big factor as far as our emotions misfiring with our brains. In my first book, I gave an example that I'd not only like to give again, but one I will expand.

We need to keep it new and fresh.

During a busy day at an office, an employee is walking down the hallway when the boss happens to be walking in the opposite direction. Remember, it is a busy day, people are coming and going. Picture a midweek late morning. The employee and the boss cross mid-hallway.

"Heya," says the employee. Or maybe, "Hi, Doctor."

The boss barely grumbles a reply, quickly walking right on by without even looking at his worker.

Through that brief interaction, the employee then gets a bunch of data for an *individual* interpretation. The employee jumps to any of these conclusions:

 "Geez, the boss hates me!"

 "I guess that last report I turned in really wasn't what he was looking for."

 "Yeah, I heard a few people were gonna be let go this week. That seals the deal. I'm definitely one of them."

Now, let's consider the data that this employee did not have—and it would be unlikely that he or should could have this data:

 On this particular day the boss was under a terrible deadline.

 The boss was about to lose a patient over some mistake that he, the boss, had managed.

 Maybe the boss was simply on his way to answer the call of nature between meetings and didn't have time to stop for a chat.

A big building block of emotional intelligence involves not mistaking data for the wrong interpretation to satiate a preconceived notion. Given all that spins through the human brain second-by-second, the schemas that have already formed each individual worldview, and the stimuli people need to surf at any one given time, it's no wonder this data misinterpretation happens daily.

However, the more aware people are of where they might potentially go in their thoughts or recognizing that insufficient information may lead to a faulty conclusion, the more people can temper the data, and therefore the interpretation. This is the big cause-and-effect of emotionally-led intellect.

For another example, allow me to share the example of a potential employee I interviewed for a position at one of my dental practices. My wife, Julie, is an executive coach. She is a certified therapist and has been instrumental in helping me build, grow, and develop my practices and run my dental resource management group. As she is a managing partner in this business, she thought it prudent for her to also meet the potential new employee. I agreed and set up a meeting, just the two of them. I went on with my day, figuring Julie would check in after their appointment, to give me her feedback.

I didn't hear from her, so I texted. I still didn't hear from Julie. I texted again. Still no reply. I continued to text her, time passed, but no answer from my wife. I grew impatient. I began to jump to a myriad of conclusions.

See what I did?

From a lack of information, or the data I had at hand—no data at all, really—I jumped to a conclusion. I interpreted. Actually, I didn't interpret a thing. I just couldn't for the life of me understand why the Julie wasn't getting back to me in the time allotted.

Yes, we do expect too much with our texting and Facebook prompting. Why hasn't that person gotten back to me? It's been a minute-and-a-half already! In this case, I was jumping around mentally.

"She isn't texting me back," I said to myself, "the interview must have really gone off the rails."

Then, I went to my sarcasm. I figured Julie was saying to herself, "Oh here we go, Steve has picked a real winner, this time!"

In my case, I had no excuse. I didn't even have data to misinterpret. See, I am a flawed human just like anybody else, and I'm well-versed in this emotional intelligence stuff.

For people predisposed to be a "Debbie Downer" about the world in general, or conversely, all Richard Simmons[9] bubbly 24/7, when you learn which you are, you've won half the battle. If you can hold your predispositions back even some of the time, then you will be operating with more awareness than most people around you as you slow down assumptions and place the data in proper perspective.

You may realize that people jump to conclusions to get on with the day, or simply because, well, people like to jump to conclusions. Human beings do their best work on either side of the fence, not sitting on it. So, even if people come to the wrong conclusion or are in mental anguish, they still have an answer they can work around.

Just remember, the answer or interpretation that any person may reach might not always be the right one for the multitude of reasons just discussed.

---

9 https://richardsimmons.com/ (if you were born after 1985, you might need this link to explain the reference)

# 5 Psychological Enemy #4: The Crazy Train

You know it's coming. You feel yourself preparing for the trip. Your mind's eye view is passing station nameplates on swinging signs as you reach around for your bags. You have come this way plenty of times, and although you never enter or leave this destination with a good feeling, you coddle a certain warm anticipation about this visit.

You know it. You've ridden it. All aboard the crazy train.

It's not so much that you feel the people or the place will have changed. In fact, you know the people can't change—and, indeed, you are counting on this fact. Yet here you are again, on the crazy train, pulling into the station, ready to embark and give flight to to all of your fears, passive aggressiveness, and schemas. Everything you need to lay waste to just about anybody is waiting for you at the station. The place has not changed.

All metaphors aside, most likely when things are going off the rails for you emotionally, you'll know it. You might not be able to determine exactly what got you hopping on the train this time, but you are on it and determined to see it to the end.

Why?

First, this is familiar territory. Even under the apparent stress for a trip of this sort, you are comforted by doing something you have done before. Nobody likes to get all riled up and crazy—unless of course, it is precisely what they are comfortable doing.

Habit? The same old script? A dash of schema? You betcha!

Second, getting truly worked up shuts down any opposition or even reasoned advice or help from a friend, spouse, or coworker. Fists clenched, crying to the point of what seems sure to be a breakdown, steaming to the point your ears redden, or screaming at the top of your lungs—really, who's going to mess with you when you're like this?

And if somebody does? Well, part of this trip is that you are usually ready for a fight.

Quite frankly, there are times when we ride the crazy train really wanting someone along for the ride. Not just for a fight, as mentioned above, but to deliberately pull someone in, grabbing onto the classic enabler who has punched your ticket time and time again or perhaps someone new you are trying to manipulate.

As we fit schemas into our grand perceptions and work out our habits, we often judge and amass our audience around us by what they bring to the table when we are at our worst. Misery loves company and so does crazy.

Lastly, whatever got you here might be something you have yet to work out, something that triggers you that you have not yet addressed or perhaps trauma you never want to face. It is much easier to roll over what ails you with a massive steam locomotive of emotion than to deal with the hard stuff. Chugging along loud and hard, you will easily miss the details, the specks under the gravel between the tracks that are the very nuggets of the problems you do not want to face yet and maybe, not ever.

The crazy train runs day and night, rain or shine, and even during holidays—and especially during holidays!

Family gatherings are great times to get pushed onto these tracks. The tracks never run out. Most people hop on and off the train whenever it suits them. And as hard as this is for me to admit this far into this wonderful change-your-life-book, even the very best emotional intelligence fanatic boards the train every now and again.

What's most interesting about going there is that usually the people around you see you board the train. The times I go spinning, Julie can often be heard saying, "Steve you should see yourself."

I know she is well aware of when I board the train…which, I hardly ever do, of course…being the super self-aware and evolved guy I am…

*Not.*

We all ride the crazy train from time to time.

The rider—the person spinning into complete abject nuttiness—doesn't notice that others see them in this way. Sometimes the rider may subconsciously cultivate relationships that they can exploit when riding their train. When someone is reacting so acutely to stress or a trigger, they are not usually in tune with anyone else's feelings. I know plenty of people who flip out first and ask questions later, and the more they do so, the better they become at sensing who will stick around to mollify them and who will quickly exit to get out of the way of the locomotive.

There is not just one kind of crazy train. I have been painting a picture of the person who is apt to lose it at a moment's notice, whether their go-to is white hot anger or on-the-floor or curled-up-into-a-full-fetal crying jag. There are also crazy trains that don't produce such startling office-stopping results but still clutch the traveler, as well as their audience, to the point that problems do occur.

Across the many years and the many practices I have owned and continue to oversee, I've witnessed so many of my more-emotional employees wondering why other employees avoid them. As I hear their various trains swish by, I really wish I had a mirror on hand.

But there is the kind of crazy train passenger who sits so far down in their seat and draws the curtain so tight that they wouldn't recognize themselves if I indeed did hold a mirror to their face. They do not display anger or shouting or crying, but this person still boards their own little-engine-that-could so often that they never notice anybody they pass standing at the stations or what they are doing to themselves.

In one of my offices, we once had to have a serious sit-down with a staff member who had worked for us for many years. While I had no real complaints about the individual's work, I had heard plenty about their attitude. This particular employee was known for rubbing everybody the wrong way and had done so for a decade. This was the kind of person that had a negative counter-statement to whatever anyone said.

Even the most mundane, "Well, it is certainly sunny today" comment would be met with a "nah, it's supposed to rain, this won't last."

After some back and forth, I realized this person would never give any ground. As much to poke the bear as to see how entrenched the individual really was, I asked: "In all these years of working here, and all of the people that you have come in contact with, would you say it has been *all of those people* who are the problem, and not you?"

Looking me in the eye, my employee responded in all seriousness: "Yes. It has always been somebody else, never me."

They truly believed that the problems were everyone else's fault. Denial is not just a river in Egypt, huh?

This person followed a specific meandering track, hopped on and off at whim, and executed a perfect, consistent journey of persecution. Maybe not the stuff of a Disneyland, wild Mr. Toad's ride of full-anger or desperation, but indeed these were unique tracks lain down over time.

Everyone wants to be able to use that count-to-ten rule of breathing deep and considering the next action. Everyone would like to give themselves a good shake every now and again and stop the slide down the rabbit hole. Everyone wants to get off the train and even, in some cases, never hop on again.

But I dare say, quite often it is a hell of a lot easier to find a seat in a compartment and let the trip head where it will, then stop, drop, and roll into some deep meditation or reasoned consideration. That old train track is always spread there, always ready for the chugging locomotive to use its track. It's up to the individual to come aboard or not. Each person has a great capacity for habits, to fold schemas to a certain worldview, to rationalize, and to bubble up passive-aggressiveness. People too easily get their tickets punched for a ride on the crazy train.

It's reasonable to assume that the more people expand their emotional intelligence, the less they might get jammed by some of this stuff. These first few chapters have shown that human biology and neuroscience are problematic determinants to overcome, but that the fight is well worth the effort to be better people, both individually and for the community.

One of the simplest ways to circumvent the problems is simply to *focus*.

I know, you're probably saying, "Sure, Dr. H., that's a hell of a lot easier said than done. Have you seen the crapola I am dealing with daily?!"

But in a very practical way, focusing aids the application of emotional intelligence, fixes attention like a laser, and shuts out the noise. Focus can take on the form of meditation, directing one's self to one task, or undertaking intense physical exertion. Any of these approaches will distract the brain from whatever stuff had it bothered in the first place.

The ability to focus is an essential skill of gathering attention. When a habit kicks in, the ability to focus helps control the teeter between data and interpretation. Focus slows the mind, allows grounding, and gathers strengths or power.

You know how it is when you are stressed, when a tremendous prejudice blocks your way, or when you feel yourself slipping back into a script you have too often played. You can almost feel your head hurting or steam leaking out your ears. Focusing allows all parts of the brain to function at their best and battles those various symptoms of psychological inertia.

I know it's not so easy to do, but focusing the mind and body together, as much as becoming aware of the developed schemas, will guide your lions, tigers, and bears, metaphorically speaking, to greater EI.

# 6 Psychological Enemy #5: Passive Aggressive Behavior

## The Passive-Aggressive Aggressor

The last thing I'd ever want to be accused of is throwing clichés your way or playing to the "cheap seats," but really, how could we get through a book about emotional intelligence without mentioning passive aggressiveness?

We have all been privy to that man or woman in the workplace or in a million other places out in the world whose primary goal in life is to hold us emotionally hostage with their seemingly benign actions and off-handed remarks. The total opposite of the nurturing side of EI, the passive-aggressive aggressor usually has one end of the EI equation down: they recognize the moods and triggers of others and know how to exploit them for their purposes.

Getting into the deep end of a relationship, we know that EI can work wonders. So much good can come from either avoiding someone's triggers or prompting them positively. But it's also important to understand that your EI can protect you. When you encounter people who confront the world with a tickle of passive-aggressiveness or those who are masters at the craft, you can use your keen sense of awareness to keep this insidious acting at bay.

It's likely you have experienced this particular behavior. You may even have perpetrated some of it yourself. It's human nature. Verbal jabs, teasing that borders on the bitingly sarcastic, silent treatment, and withholding intimacy (from a spouse or not being warm and friendly to a friend or sibling) are all classic examples of passive aggressiveness.

One might sabotage a colleague's project "accidentally" or respond with "I'm fine" when they are anything but fine. There is so much in the passive-aggressive toolbox.

No matter what the bad behavior is, the passive-aggressive individual is usually disguising their manipulation until they feel you are rightly schooled. All attention is on them, just as they wish it to be.

So, why do they—or we as humans—act this way? Why not just come out and say what is on our minds?

Well, this is learned behavior here, folks. We don't come out of the womb being passive-aggressive. Somewhere in our life we learn that acting this way, although not very nice, has gotten us something we want. Recognizing and understanding *why* is at the root of stopping this behavior in ourselves, as well as in battling passive-aggressive transgressors.

## Where It Comes From: Attachment Insecurity

Some family dynamics and the encounters and experiences of childhood will often result in passive-aggressive behavior in adults. A domineering family member could cause undue contention in the home, for example. Often a person in a subservient role comes to rely on covert passive-aggressive tendencies in order to gain the edge over their bully. Additionally, if someone witnesses passive-aggressiveness as a child, and notes the effectiveness of the behavior, they could certainly learn to cultivate this behavior.

Similarly, *attachment insecurity* might evolve in a budding passive-aggressor. This is a problem born from loved ones leaving or disappointing a person time and time again. They come to feel that those that they love and need will not stay around or be there for them. Born from this specific neglected childhood experience, the passive-aggressor will act out in adulthood, hoping that their victim will come to value them the way they were never valued in their youth. The persons the passive-aggressor picks, be they lover, co-worker, or friends, are often substitutes for whomever actually *did* leave the aggressor in the past. By acting out, the aggressor forces people to stick around.

Conversely, the passive-aggressor with an attachment insecurity might also display an aversion to closeness. In effect, what they want so very badly, they are unable to give. If the passive-aggressor was unduly mocked for something they could do nothing about—a physical oddity, supposed lack of intellect, or sexual preference, for instance—they might have grown up wanting openly to punish society. They manage to do so without showing themselves, operating under a veil of passive-aggressive acts. Instead of screaming, biting, or kicking against those who have done them wrong, they lash out under cover of benign and seemingly positive behavior.

Overall, passive-aggressive behavior is cultivated and wielded when someone feels powerless. A passive-aggressor might become more so when faced with losing a position at work or trying to hide an error or ignorance. I have heard of plenty of older dentists trying to cover up their lack of technological knowledge by throwing verbal jabs at younger doctors and even deliberately sabotaging procedures.

Regardless of the source of the aggression, the person pulling these stunts is doing so for one reason: personal gain. Whether it be a better position at work, to sabotage you, to have you pay an inordinate amount of attention to them, or to test your loyalty or caring—it is all about exerting some control on the world, gaining advantage, or salving a wound.

## Stopping Passive Aggressiveness in Others

The key to halting passive-aggressiveness is to first to become aware of it and then to confront it. Passive-aggressiveness is bullying at its simplest level. When you stand up to someone who is attempting to lay a passive-aggressive trip on you, you take away their power.

First and foremost, *do not be fooled*. It is mighty easy to be duped. By its very nature, passive-aggressiveness is covert, seeming the opposite of what it is, and often delivered with a smile and sweetness.

Remember, all passive-aggressive behavior is a form of hostility even if the person doing it is hurting. The aggressor has an agenda, and they are out to get exactly what they want without revealing their motives or needs. Keep this in mind when the person you confront is smiling or claiming they are sorry for being a few minutes late, as they always are.

The biggest mistake we can make is to give passive-aggressive behavior a pass or give in to it. Give the perpetrator an inch, and they will most certainly take a mile. If you excuse or allow this kind of manipulation, even once, get ready for plenty more.

Remember, each time your aggressor gets to play you, the stronger their methods become, and the more they will play their games. You need to shut them down quickly, and the only way to do this is to realize you are in the throes of it.

Then you must *confront* the behavior. This is not as easy as it sounds, especially in an office environment. Calling out a co-worker on their B.S. can cause ripples across the tranquil waters of your place of business, drench co-workers, and even manage to sprinkle some drops on customers—our patients.

Of course, the passive-aggressor is hoping for this. They want attention and to be seen as the ultimate victim. All the world's indeed a stage for them. Go ahead! Make your opposition to them as vocal as you like. This is what they want. Confrontation takes some finesse, to be sure.

I suggest a one-on-one meeting when facing this person and addressing the issue. This way, you can have your say without distractions and keep things discreet and concise. If your aggressor wants to yell foul, back-peddle, or even cry, the only one they'll end up performing for is you, if you stick around long enough for their reaction. And, you shouldn't. Sure, listen well to the passive-aggressor, but don't be their punching bag.

You also need to *be kind* here and compassionate. I know, you're probably mighty upset at the aggressor as well as at yourself for letting all this fester for so long. Try to rise above your anger. Yes, this person may have dug a great rift between you and they may have set the entire office on edge, holding everybody emotionally hostage and causing you to twist and turn in knots trying to please them.

But, as previously noted, they are also hurting. Something is lacking for them. Insecurity is at the root of their behaviors. You need not be judgmental or adopt a harsh or negative tone. Don't stoop to the level of the aggressor.

Another good game to play—and I hate making this all about game playing, but sometimes the best way to deal with a person who plays these emotional games is play right along with them—*is to act dumb.*

Admittedly, I have often been accused that I'm not acting here, but if someone gives you the classic gambit: "No, go ahead, I'm fine" or perpetrates that other gem of being late just take them at their word or action. Don't read or react any deeper. Play stupid. If someone says that they are fine, then assume they are, and act according to what they say.

If they are late, let them face the consequences. If you told everyone to meet at 7:30 to leave for a movie, leave at 7:35. If they whine to you later, tell them simply: "Sorry, the movie started at 8, I told you we were leaving at 7:30."

Just as you do with straight-on confrontation, responding simply in your reactions, so simply that you might even seem dense or stupid, cuts the legs off of many a passive-aggressor.

You can also *set limits* on possible actions before they occur. A simple "I never wait any longer than five minutes for anybody" or "sorry, if any co-worker doesn't open their email within two days of receipt, they will miss out on those extra jobs when they come up." The onus is on you here, so you'll need to make good on the promise of your limits. Follow through with your follow through! The minute you let your defenses down and let a rule slide, the passive-aggressor will inevitably slide into the opening you have allowed. Don't kid yourself, these folks live and die on how well and how often they can manipulate those around them. They are always studying angles.

This leads to another, critical point when shutting down passive-aggressive behavior: *be specific.* Address the person by answering precisely what they said or did, avoid generalities or sweeping statements like "you always do such and such" or "you are late with assignments every single time." When you finally confront them, even if indeed you are addressing their hostile habits, address the most recent offense. Again, *be specific.*

If your passive-aggressor is especially adept at revising history to meet their needs, claiming they never heard what you said or twisting your words and meanings, you can quickly stop this behavior. Bring another person in with you when you come to meet your passive-aggressive co-worker and tell them that since there is consistent misunderstanding, you are going to have another person sit in so there is no more miscommunication.

I have unfortunately been in situations where this is the only way to deal with someone trying to pull the wool over my eyes. This method, more than any other, will halt the madness, and the passive-aggressor has no wiggle room if you are taking the step to make sure you get every word down verbatim. This is a drastic measure though, so best done behind closed doors.

If you have the time, the desire, and the kind of relationship with the passive-aggressor where you can sit them down for a calm discussion, then bring all of your emotional intelligence to bear and see if you can get to the meat of the matter. Try to address the real reason this person has to go through all these time-wasting, soul-sucking, possibly friendship-killing modes of behavior.

If you can break someone of this habit things will undoubtedly be better in your relationship. Though decidedly this is not your job, even as a friend or family member, and indeed not as a co-worker, employer, or employee. The overall lesson is to be aggressive in a kind, but firm, manner. You need to be confident, direct, and on-point with your words and actions when dealing with people playing the passive-aggressive stance with you.

## Stopping Passive Aggressive Behavior In Yourself

Yes, I know, you are just too self-aware. You are God's gift to your office, friends, and family. You would *never* be passive-aggressive. But for those of us not made of starlight and Skittles (although how much goodness can be in a Skittle if they are now banned in both Europe and California), how do we avoid being passive-aggressive?

In two words: *Don't be!*

The actions taken here are yours to accept or not. As you build your emotional intelligence and get to know yourself better, you will awaken an inner mindfulness that will bring you more in tune with your feelings and reactions. With a heightened sense of awareness, you honestly will have no reason to go forth and be passive-aggressive. You will have a quicker understanding of where your anger comes from and therefore be able to control it. You will grow a deeper connection to your co-workers, understanding their moods, and when they are reaching out to you. You'll come to realize how important it is that you respond positively, and to help and share and support people rather than trying to knock them down or twist them up.

Most importantly, you'll be able to sniff out potential situations that could cause you stress and fear. You will have the emotional tools to avoid them or confront them head-on. And you will be more willing to reach out for help, guidance, and support for yourself.

This awareness will do the one thing a passive-aggressive aggressor can't do—it'll forever keep your head out of your keister. One of the biggest enemies of building razor-sharp emotional intelligence is letting your ego grow to the point where you don't recognize anybody else on the planet!

But don't worry, this particular symptom might not be your fault…

## The Modern World Feeds the Passive Aggressive

Ok, I lied—it is your fault. Did you think that after reading the initial pages in this book, I'd let you get away with not owning your words, deeds, and emotions?

The ego you grow is your own. It is up to you to deal with it. Given what we are up against in the modern world, it is very easy to fertilize an out-of-control sense of self-worth and pretty damn easy to let passive-aggressiveness fly loose, untamed, and hardly ever confronted.

Think about this on the most basic level. Anyone can tweet, post, or text anything they're feeling in the moment.

To passive-aggressors, this open forum for opinions is like opium to an addict. In years past, aggressors had to hold their thoughts until they had a live, and often captive, audience. With the instant gratification of social media and smart phones, they can now say anything they wish the minute they feel it and the consequences be damned! The more passive-aggressive you are, the more consequences you're looking for, no?

Plenty of people no longer dial their phone but opt to communicate by text. Others relate their latest news by posting on social media or bark their feelings at you across the web, not caring a wit for your response. People display memes and quotes to let the world in on their feelings, knowing they can put whatever they want out there. The internet is the deepest sandbox for the passive-aggressor, with quips, jokes, pictures, and sayings that are perfect for hiding real intent.

It's a one-way conversation, a daily regurgitation of letting everyone in on our mindset and emotional state, without having to be ever accountable for the spreading negativity all over the world.

Later, I will take a deeper dive into modern social media and how it is the true enemy of emotional intelligence. But take it on faith that nothing in the last twenty years has helped the cause of passive-aggressiveness better than social media. The last thing the person playing passive-aggressive games wants is for you to have your day in court, to be able to air your true feelings of how you feel manipulated by them. All they want is for you to fall for their B.S. consistently and to know they have you on the hook. The world wide web allows them everything they need to continue this one-way conversation.

And here's another tip how to shut down the passive-aggressor in your midst: block their number, unfriend them, unfollow their social accounts.

Yeah, I know, you fear you might miss something in this great big world of ours if you don't catch your co-worker's last Instagram post, but in the most basic application of all martial arts: *If you are not there to receive the strike, you won't get struck.*

## The Passive-Aggressive Reactionary

I've so far highlighted the person who makes your life difficult by what they do to you, either before or during some forward motion you are trying to bring off. Still, there are plenty of passive-aggressors who pull their stunts after the fact, as a reaction to something that has gone on. In a way, all passive-aggressiveness is a reaction of sorts, but I'm referring here to the person who reacts passive-aggressively directly after something happens.

The silent treatment is perfect for this. You anger the passive-aggressor, and they shut down. Now, I am all for considering your thoughts, actions, and words well before you react. After all, the primary tenet of emotional intelligence is the "count to ten" rule. It is something we should all be applying in our daily routine.

Unfortunately, the passive-aggressive reactionary uses this technique in a way to directly punish people. Sure, I know plenty of couples who ache for the silent treatment when their spouse gets going on a point. They ache for their partner shutting up about that one point they are going on and on about!

But for our purposes here, the seasoned aggressor is purposefully not talking so as to stretch your nerves. They want you to seek them out, to goad them into speaking. They are trying to get and keep your attention, rather than telling you what you might have done that has upset them. They want you to beg them to discuss what you are keeping mum about by keeping mum until you can't stand it.

How to stop it? Don't stick around for it. Do not mollify or address.

## Passive-Aggressiveness Applied to the Office

It's no real stretch to see how passive-aggressive behavior will undermine office harmony. It will rip our medical code of ethics asunder, cause friction between staff, patients, and dentists, and bring undue stress into the practice. I'd like to think that all of us working in a dental practice would keep passive-aggressive behavior out of our daily doings, or quickly nip it in the bud, but such is not always the case. Out of all the unproductive maneuvers a person might attempt (whether person means a patient, doctor, nurse, accountant, or ourselves), passive-aggressive behavior is the most insidious and destructive.

We see it in staff members who refuse to perform even the most mundane task or make those tasks unnecessarily more difficult. We see it as the classic "us-against-them" posture between staff and patients, in the eye-rolling when Mr. or Mrs. Patient So-and-So (and those damned So-and-So kids!) sign in. We see it over long-term care when a doctor or staff member has encountered a difficult patient time and again, but can no longer surf that patient's particular quirks. We see it trickling down when staff members deliberately sabotage work to make a manager, or even a doctor, look bad.

The thing to remember here is that any behavior that may interfere with patient safety or the better workings of a dental office cannot be tolerated. Developing good emotional intelligence allows you to recognize and stop this B.S. And passive-aggressive behaviors are the kind of B.S. a razor-sharp dental practice cannot support!

Of course, what you do in one place, you'll do everywhere. This is true for most of human behavior. It does not exist in a vacuum. I know people like to think they are great at compartmentalizing, wearing one face at work and another with family. Even if we can play Dr. Jekyll most of the time, Mr. Hyde is bound to make an appearance occasionally.

You know as well as I do that if you are not feeling your best mentally, it tends to show on you physically. If you are twisted up from something like back pain or stuffed up from allergies, your mood can be affected. The same is true in the bigger picture of your life. I rarely, if ever, have seen the employee who can come into the office, spread some good vibes among my patients and their fellow staff members, be pretty much a rock star worker, and yet be suffering a terrible home life. Admittedly, some people can hide certain parts of their life from others well, but over time what is happening in one aspect of your life, tearing at or bolstering your emotions, seeps in to affect another part.

If you are passive-aggressive at the office, most probably you are also showering your family with the same bad vibe.

I don't wish any of this time-wasting silliness on anybody, and I certainly don't ever want to see you resort to this behavior because you feel insecure. Cultivate a deep emotional intelligence and you will be able to battle passive-aggressiveness from others, as well as in yourself.

# 7 The History of Emotional Intelligence

Back when cavemen and women were trying to keep a fire going, maintaining order in the cave, and hunting and gathering to ensure the family had enough to eat, they relied more on instinct than intelligence to survive. But follow human evolution a little further up the chain, and we find that big brain philosophers—Plato, Aristotle, Descartes—began to consider emotional responses and stimuli.

These brilliant minds considered the reasons humans did things and how they might do them better. Lots of study through the centuries has gone into man beating back his emotions with his intellect, but generally, there has always been a school of thought that has factored emotional intelligence into the mix, even before there was a name for it. Big brain or small, philosopher or theologian, guy or gal, humanity as a species has come to realize that the head and the heart are linked, both pushing and pulling all the time.

In the 1930s, Edward Thorndike[10] defined *social intelligence* as the ability to get along with others, and David Wechsler[11] furthered his concept by suggesting that the moods, feelings, and attitudes surrounding intelligence could be critical components to success. Abraham Maslow[12] got the 50s going with his idea that humans could build emotional strength. Imagine that—not only do humans have emotional strength, but by exercising it, humans could improve themselves in this area.

We are pretty amazing creatures when we put our mind to it, huh?

In 1975, Howard Gardner introduced multiple intelligence theories[13] in his book *The Shattered Mind*[14]. Ten years later, Wayne Payne titled his

---

10 https://www.goodtherapy.org/famous-psychologists/edward-thorndike.html
https://www.goodtherapy.org/famous-psychologists/edward-thorndike.html
11 https://www.hellovaia.com/explanations/psychology/famous-psychologists/david-wechsler/
12 https://webspace.ship.edu/cgboer/maslow.html
13 https://files.eric.ed.gov/fulltext/ED618540.pdf
14 https://openlibrary.org/books/OL5203300M/The_shattered_mind
https://www.amazon.com/Shattered-Mind-Howard-Gardner/dp/0394719468

## EI Resources
Following are some invaluable resources for continuing your education on EI.

**http://www.eiconsortium.org**
The Consortium for Research on emotional intelligence in Organizations (CREIO) is devoted to keeping up on all the latest tidbits, studies, and events relevant to EI. Listing podcasts, articles, video, and schedules for speaker engagements, this is one of the many portals in existence that is cultivating the worldview of EI and how it is vitally important to us all. It's interesting to note that CREIO was first established to release and study information about EI in the workplace.

**http://ei.yale.edu**
You can visit Yale Center for emotional intelligence for a purely educational stop. (Remember Peter Salovey and John Mayer taught and met at Yale.)

**https://e-ii.org**
The non-profit Emotional Intelligent Institute (EII) was founded in 2001, and offers free lessons and a self-study program to help improve emotional literacy.

doctoral dissertation, "A Study of Emotion: Developing Emotional Intelligence; Self-Integration; Relating to Fear, Pain, and Desire."[15] In 1990, Yale Professor Peter Salovey and his colleague, Professor John Mayer, of the University of New Hampshire, developed the idea of what is defined today as emotional intelligence[16], all while painting the walls of Salovey's house. Salovey studied emotions and behavior, and Mayer studied the link between emotions and thought.

It's ironic that what seems so obvious now, and was indeed considered for centuries, didn't slip into any real modern theorizing until Salovey and Mayer in the 1990s. Each coming from his own area of specialty, the painting buddies published their theory in the *Imagination, Cognition, and Personality* journal. Three years later, Dr. Daniel Goleman (referenced earlier), working then as a science reporter for *The New York Times*, stumbled across Salovey and Mayer. He went on to give their theory a more wide-reaching airing in his 1995 book *Emotional Intelligence: Why It Can Matter More Than IQ.* That provocative first book was the first real mainstream exposure of EI.

With all the self-help avenues we have access to becoming ever more prominent, including tools like executive and life coaching, to which I presently devote my professional life, the concept of emotional intelligence is widely accepted. While folks today seem very focused on conversations about artificial intelligence (AI), I feel it is doubly important to keep our eye

15 https://philpapers.org/rec/PAYASO
16 https://journals.sagepub.com/doi/10.2190/DUGG-P24E-52WK-6CDG (original article)

on the ball where EI is concerned. I believe that when the potential and the possible AI demonstrated by machines is upon us, it will be a considerable cause for human emotional intelligence to step up….in fact, it should be stepping up, right now!

Sure, machines can calculate faster, provide for safety, and facilitate many programs to run at the same time but they cannot replicate the nuances needed or engender the understanding required when two or more human beings interact. While we rely on machines and technology all the time in our diagnosis and treatments, a patient cannot be put at ease by a machine. A computer cannot display a bedside manner; commiserate, console, and explain; or read a patient's facial expression, body language, or speech patterns. Only another human can sufficiently put another human at ease.

Machines also cannot lead. They can't woo a crowd or stand as an example to a troop. They cannot take the emotional temperature of a room or determine whether to call a break in a heated discussion or to push when solutions are nearing. They cannot empathize, influence, or level employees with a healthy dose of civility when staff is overworked and stressed.

We EI-ers have nothing to fear from the future!

# 8 Why Emotional Intelligence is Vital in Our Practice

Let's not forget. This is a book about building an emotionally intelligent dental practice.

Cultivating an office environment of people aware of one another's moods and trying to create positive interaction amongst staff, patients, and referring doctors is extremely valuable. Fostering a good feeling throughout the dental practice should make the practice all the more pleasant. And this is also good for business.

But even understanding this, offices don't always make for the best EI Petri dishes unless the people, especially those in supervisory or ownership roles, work hard at making them so.

Beyond these obvious goals there are more concrete reasons why emotional intelligence is so important in a dental practice:

- EI creates a team.
- EI cultivates learning.
- EI can predict.
- EI helps with recruitment as well as retention.
- EI also helps when firing someone.
- EI creates stability for staff, patients, and referring dentists.
- EI cultivates self-regulation and self-management.
- EI thwarts gossip and backstabbing.
- EI makes your office unique to you.

**EI creates a team.** It's simple logic that if everyone is getting along at the office, or at least has a modicum of caring and understanding of one another's particular idiosyncrasies, that practice will have a more harmonious working unit. Staff will be less prone to flare-ups, manipulations, trying to undercut one another, or vying for the attention of the boss (yeah, I know I'm wonderful but...)

I won't kid you. It's impossible for everybody to get along as much as it is impossible for everyone to be aware of, and even care about, each other's feelings. However, if there is even the *smallest* sense of a team unit, or a family-staff sensibility, it will make for a more harmonious work environment. Emotional intelligence grows this kind of one-for-all feeling.

*Be careful though.* Time and again, I have to remind people that bettering your EI does not change you. People who are new to this concept or bristle against it often feel as if joining in on simple decency, politeness, and maybe a little personal discourse every so often is akin to drinking the Kool-Aid, becoming entrenched in a culture and losing one's identity.

Nothing could be farther from the truth. With emotional intelligence, bosses and workers are using more insight than ever before to right the ship and keep things afloat with more awareness.

**EI cultivates learning.** There are constant teachable and learning moments happening. The better employees' emotional awareness, the more possibility there is that they will learn as well as teach. A boss wants to have their staff find their own pace and open their minds as they see fit to skills, opinions, and innovations. It's imperative that people feel that their emotions are protected, valued, and nurtured. In this environment, everyone will take the extra step, not just go through the motions in procedures. They will jump at the chance to take a class or to learn something out of their immediate comfort zone or job when the environment is ripe for learning and caring.

*Another note of caution:* In some instances, it is imperative that staff learns something new or takes a class out of the office. The healthy work environment might indeed be one where people want to learn, but compulsory learning is not always an easy pill to swallow even with the best intentions swirling around. Nobody wants to feel they are being made to go back to school or being treated like the child who needs to learn something.

In my first book, *The Dentist Who Gets It*, I cited Marissa Ann Mayer, who served as president of the web-portal services company Yahoo! from 2012 to 2017, and something she tried with her employees. Combatting what seemed to be a pattern of less and less time her remote staffers were putting in, Mayer made everyone come into the office to work. Attempting to address the problem of a lackluster home-work ethic, this tactic only served to build resentment in her staff and showed her weakness in not being able to find what the staff considered a reasonable solution to a problem. Not only did Mayer engender some queasy feelings forcing her workers back into the office, but suddenly she created an 'us' against 'her' situation where no one would ever go out on a limb for her again.

**EI can predict.** If a dental office works with a high level of awareness, everyone should be able to predict possible storms on the horizon. Staff won't be so frequently ambushed by a referring dentist's ire, a fellow employee's resentment, or a disgruntled patient. If the team is aware of one another's moods, if one of your staff can get on the phone with a regularly referring dentist and tell from his or her tone when they have a problem before they even articulate it, or if your receptionist can take the temperature of the waiting room just by the body language of a handful of patients sitting there, then the staff should be able to brace themselves for, or even prevent, negative encounters. At the very least, the boss could be alerted that there might soon be a problem he has to address.

Remember though, good office emotional intelligence does not make us budding Nostradamus-es (or is the plural of Nostradamus, Nostradamus-i?). Still, better awareness certainly makes our senses more acute.

**EI helps with recruitment as well as retention.** I find that one of my biggest difficulties in maintaining the practices I do, is not so much worrying about the day-to-day actions of my staff but the hiring and retaining of staff. It's happened on more than one occasion that my gut reaction has helped me hire somebody who turns out to be a fantastic member of my team. Listening to my gut has also prevented me from hiring somebody who looks great on paper but, for some reason, gave me a bad vibe.

Retention is another piece of this puzzle. If an employee thinks they have found a better fit, then I wish them God's speed. However, cultivating a healthy and happy home base means very few of my people want to leave.

The downside? Well, I personally have been waylaid by my feelings for someone versus their performance record or their actual work. There is a fine line between going with your gut and having your gut cloud your judgment. In a perfect world or a high-functioning EI dental practice, a trusted staff member or manager might sniff out the stuff you haven't and alert you to poor performance after you hire someone or give them a raise.

**EI also helps when firing someone.** Contrary to hiring and retention, one of the worst parts of being a boss is letting a staff member go. In a dental practice, which is essentially a small business, this affects us all harder than it would at a big corporation. But it has got to be done sometimes.

Quite frankly, when you have your emotional intelligence honed you are more able to hike up your britches and do even the most unpleasant of tasks. That's not to say that a firing doesn't sting or that it can't become very personal, but each case is individual. Be it your manager, head dentist, you, or anyone else who might need to perform this uncomfortable necessity, emotional intelligence will serve everyone when firing someone.

*Here is how I would do it:* You should rehearse the firing to soften the blow and deliver it truthfully. You need to set up a safe, private space for these difficult one-on-one meetings. There are also times when the boss or manager needs to have a second person in the office on the firing. If you're not sure this is one of those cases, ask someone to join you. Better safe than sorry. Your office protocol as well as your emotional intelligence will help you determine how to proceed.

But do not make this moment more than it has to be.

Let's be honest: this isn't something anyone likes, no matter which side of the desk you're sitting on. Having a good sense of yourself and being prepared will help ensure that you do not go back on your intention, nor be swayed or played. Preparedness is a nice symptom of EI. Use it well in this instance.

It's safe to assume that the mood is going to be negative, even if the employee expects you are lowering the boom this day. Anticipating someone else's mood will help you surf the outburst, if it comes, and mollify, if given the opportunity.

In some cases, it will do you and your ex-employee good to air precisely why he or she did not work out. In other instances, where there might be a clash of personalities causing the firing, it might be best to remain silent beyond the actual firing discussion. The thing with becoming more aware is that you will be able to fashion your response to whatever is needed to diffuse this powder keg of a situation.

**EI creates stability for staff, patients, and referring dentists.** As mentioned earlier, a healthy work environment sees less staff turnover, and builds a staff that works more seamlessly the more time they spend working together. (More on referring dentists in an upcoming chapter. No peeking!)

**EI cultivates self-regulation and self-management.** This is where I come to see the real day-to-day application of emotional intelligence. A staff supporting one another can self-manage and self-regulate themselves better than anything I could ever bring to bear. The more they self-regulate, the better they get at it. So, why not set them free to cultivate an environment of self-management?

Sometimes the way to encourage emotional intelligence is just to let it work.

**EI thwarts gossip and backstabbing.** Other than passive aggressiveness, I haven't witnessed anything that undermines an office like gossip. Unfortunately, this is almost the bedrock of too many workplaces, not just dental offices.

And truthfully, I have learned lots about what is going on around the office by lending an ear when two workers don't know I'm listening. But generally, gossip seeps in like termites into a wooden barn and eats away at the structure bit-by-bit.

So, with good emotional intelligence, problems and personality friction are faced quickly, and things are not given ground to fester. Somebody that's even slightly self-aware is more apt to search for resolutions when they encounter conflicts or gossip.

**EI makes your office unique to you.** Do I need to tell you how many providers there are in your area that do the work that you do? I'm a specialist and I see new endodontists'offices popping up every day.

Running a successful dental practice requires both recruiting new patients and keeping them. When I first got into the business, dentists didn't talk about advertising. These days, who doesn't have a website? How many have a billboard?

The competition is fierce, and I can tell you this with no fear of contradiction: the more emotional intelligence you have flying around, the better things will be for your bottom line. If you want to make this just about dollars and cents, so be it. The truth is you will gain and retain patients at a higher rate, the more emotionally intelligent your office is.

At the heart of a feel-good office with a staff who treats patients nicely is the fact that emotional intelligence makes an office and its workers special. Even if that practice down the hallway in that spacious suite has dentists who are tapped into their EI, that group of guys and gals are not utilizing their EI in precisely the same way your staff is.

That's the benefit here: EI boosts the best of each individual. No two people and no two offices will ever be the same.

Certainly, none of this will work if it's not applied. If a manager, boss, or even somebody who has a smidgen of seniority over others doesn't walk the talk of a self-aware human, it will be tough to implement emotional intelligence in the office.

I often say we should not aim to be travel agents in life. A travel agent is great at recommending places to go, can arrange a car rental, hotel, and flights, but often when a client asks for details about the spot the travel agent is booking for the client, the usual reply is, "Oh, I don't really know, I've never been there."

You want your boss, co-worker, or friend to "have been there," living EI on a regular basis. I try every day to be the best boss I can be, as well as the best father and husband. To me, this is the most important work I can and should be doing.

# 9 Emotional Intelligence and Referred Patients & Referring Dentists

These days, patients find dentists as much from online reviews or by being attracted to neatly-rendered websites or from the old-fashioned recommendations from friends and family. Reputation travels far, and yes, there are times when one dentist will refer a patient to another. In the endodontic and oral surgery offices I lead, and even during my tenure working full-time on patients, I'd say almost all of my patients come to my practices via some sort of referral.

You can assume then that I want to apply my emotional intelligence with the doctors referring patients to me as much as to those new patients.

### Patients Who Are Referred

Here we have the classic can't un-ring a bell, "you don't get a second chance to make a first impression" moment. Applying some awareness and empathy to the guy or gal, little boy or girl, or those wacky teens who are stepping into or even calling one of my offices for the first time is imperative. This is why it's so important to have the person who answers the phone or sits at reception be not just your best representative, but a knowledgeable one at that. Pretty much the first person a patient sees or speaks to should have all the knowledge.

And I don't mean only knowledgeable about doctor's schedules and office rates. Let me explain. (And you know we're going to get to emotional intelligence.)

I always figured if the person at the front office was nice, amiable, polite, and even on the ball slightly—and I truly always try to find employees with these basic qualities—I'd be covered.

BUT the lesson I learned was that just because someone is nice and can spin through appointments quickly, does *not* mean they have a great huge amount of E.I.

I saw this played out in real time when we began to consider the percentage of people who first called us and actually made an appointment or came in for the one they initially made. We all too soon realized that numbers were not converting as well as we wanted them to.

What was the reason? In this instance it wasn't a question of patients coming in for a service and never coming back again (something that happens to every dentist, no matter what follow up procedure a patient might still need). No, we weren't even getting the referred patient to come in or go any further than speaking to the receptionist, beyond getting some quick information, then hanging up.

I knew I needed a bigger brain on this than mine.

As I will humbly state time and again, and surely a direct result of bolstering my E.I., I tend to know enough that when I don't know something, I need to get someone in who does. We called in a company called Patient Prism. They led us through their well-honed research where not only were our incoming calls monitored, but Patient Prism agents recorded and graded those incoming calls.

What we learned was astounding.

Amassing a spreadsheet log of about eighty calls in their time with us—a library of what we call the good, the bad and the ugly—it became apparent rather quickly that what patients want first and foremost when they call, is pretty much what spouses tell each other all the time that they most want when they argue: to be seen, heard and understood.

A patient wants their dilemma, pain, worry, nervousness acknowledged by the person they are talking to, even if they know, that this person's main job is to gather information and book their appointment.

Conversely, the receptionist needs to realize that being hyper-focused on getting the detailed information—who the referring dentist is, what procedure they are calling to see us for, insurance information etc.—will not improve the outcome for the patient or the office. While important facts when making an appointment, these details cannot be the primary question the new patient hears from a representative at a dental office.

When a patient calls, suffering through some discomfort or worry or offering a hasty "My son is in so much pain, please get him in as quickly possible," that person wants sympathy. That caller needs an individual on the other end of the line who sounds like they understand as much as they want to help.

Basically, as we all want from the person we tell our woes to, the patient wants an acknowledgment of what he/she are feeling and our receptionist needs to be trained as much in what words to say to acknowledge them, applying that old 'active listening.' When someone calls in crying, is in a high state of anxiety, and clearly overwhelmed with need for a dentist from my office, first and foremost the person we have answering the phone must say—is trained to say actually—"I am sorry to hear that you are in such pain" or a simple, "I am sorry to hear you are going through this."

Easy, right?

You'd be surprised.

What we do now, post Patient Prism's investigation, is have all new receptionists, during their training, sit and listen to incoming phone calls and how we handle them. You would not believe how much they learn, as we all have learned from this process.

I know it is hard to see, but we must remember that from endodontists to teeth-cleaning technicians to your family DDS, what we do is alchemy to most folks.

Yes, they can read up on procedures in *Web*MD. I have found that most of our referring dentists explain rather well why they are referring a patient to us. But still, even if most people have a rudimentary understanding, that understanding can fly out the window when someone hears that they have to see another dentist, and a specialist at that, for a further procedure!

And we all know, just hearing the word procedure is enough to cause heart palpitations in so many people.

Beyond the receptionist, it should be obvious by now how best to treat our patients, but even I have forgotten from time to time to apply a little extra effort. Let me just drop a few pearls of wisdom in this regard, take them as you may.

I heard this first one early on, as maybe you have (but it bears repeating): *patients don't care how much you know, until they know how much you care.* When someone walks out of place of business, they don't much care about the specifics of what you did and what materials you did it with, as that they would like to know their dentist or mechanic or hair dresser is happy with the work they did.

A little "I'm very happy with how this came out." or "So, how does it feel?" works wonders.

And please, if you are going to duck out of the room for any reason, make sure a nurse comes in to assure the patient that you will be right back, to bolster their confidence that everything is going smoothy.

As Maya Angelou said: "I've learned that people will forget what you said, people will forget what you did, but people will never forget how you made them feel."

This applies to all of us. Especially to us fearsome dentists.

## Doctors Who Refer Us

If I have said it once, I have said it a thousand times. The dentists who refer patients to us are our bread and butter, and I couldn't appreciate them more. And I hope that I apply my E.I. in showing these dentists how much my staff and I appreciate them.

First of all, everyone on my staff, not just the receptionists in this instance, do our best to be available to referring dentists in the best ways we can. Allowing for their schedules, I make sure that the endodontists who work for me know that if a referring dentist wants to speak to them directly, they make the time to talk to that dentist.

I also ensure to make myself available and approachable to any dentist outside of the ones who work for me. Although I don't really work as an endodontist anymore, I make it a point to attend conferences and dental networking events as much as I do meetings of corporation owners in my area. I want the other professionals in our field to marry a face with a name when they think of me, my dentists, and the work we do.

I have two sons who are very involved in hockey (yes, they get all their amazing athleticism from me...NOT). Their games continue to take me far and wide, and I do my best in my travels as much to cheer my boys on as to get out and about at any dental-based meet-ups and business talks in the area as I can.

We also work hard to have our referring dentists' backs. By this, I simply mean, no matter what a patient may say or think about the dentist who referred them to us, we always maintain a high level of professionalism, even in the face of complaints. I'm not actually saying there are any of these—really the dentists we work with are all top notch—but occasionally a patient will come in looking for a sympathetic ear over some criticism they want to level about their referring dentist. It could be complaints about how much they are being charged for visits or that their DDS just doesn't have the best bedside manner.

Often, a patient starts to talk to one of our doctors during their procedure (best they can talk during one) about whether or not what their referring dentist sent them to us for is even necessary, as if the patient is looking for a second opinion. In all these instances, my staff only ever presents a positive point of view. We simply do not dime out the referring dentist, always leading with, "Oh yes, we have heard good things about that dentist," as opposed to telling the patient flat our that this DDS isn't known for his crown work.

It's not that we aren't honest, it's just if pushed for a direct response to a patient's concern or query, we do our best to offer a morsel of something positive about the dentist they might be complaining about or try to get them back to thinking about what they are leaning back in our chair for.

Frankly, the patient's business, personal or any other with their referring dentist, is indeed their business. As mentioned earlier, one of the strengths of advancing your Emotional Intelligence is when to apply it, and when not, knowing when to get involved as much as knowing when doing so will not help a situation.

### How Much Can't Really Be Too Much

I'm reminded of that old T.V. commercial for Kellogg's Raisin Bran cereal. In that commercial, this particular cereal was touted as being the best of its kind because it had two big heaping scoops of raisins. But really how many raisins is that? How big are those scoops?

What I mean is, being nice, cordial, and caring is all well and good. You and your staff should be all these things, but how heavy are your scoops of these aspects of E.I.?

They should be heavy indeed.

The one thing I can remember from reading Dr. Stephen R. Covey's famous *The 7 Habits of Highly Effective People* is where he writes, "begin with the end in mind."

Patients and referring doctors might be coming to us for a first time or simply dealing with us every so often, but no matter how or why they come to us, when they do, we should color their initial contact with how we want them to leave us—satisfied, happy and knowing that they were cared for.

# 10 Emotional Intelligence Can Change Office Climate
## Applying what we've learned

Now, let's have a look at five of the worst boss types there are, the same archetypes found in the worst teacher, parent, manager, brother, sister, and spouse. (Of course, I am not any of these.)

**1. The string puller.** Easy to define, not so easy to work with. This is the classic micro-manager. They override every aspect of the office, home, or school, acting as the ultimate marionette master. Usually, these control freaks are set in their spirit-numbing ways because they are insecure about losing control. But that's the thing with control—just like Jell-O®, the more you try and grab it the more it slips from your grasp. I am not advising that a boss, manager, or parent should not take the reins or impress upon others what they are expecting. But one must also let their employees make mistakes and think for themselves.

**2. The string "pulled."** I know you've seen this type. This is the parent who acts more like a friend to their children than a parent, the boss who goes along with everything any employee says, or the teacher who wants to rap more than teach. Amiableness is a very endearing quality, but being a pushover, not so much. Employees, kids, and even spouses want bosses to demonstrate some backbone. People grow resentful toward someone they can walk all over even when they benefit from the walking.

**3. Stomper/gobbler.** As with the puppet master in the string puller example above, this is the boss who comes in and not only controls everyone with a heavy hand but ends up doing everything themselves. They gobble everything in sight and stomp over everything. It's one thing to have a practice run under the climate that a boss must work hard to create, but it's another to browbeat employees to the degree that the boss ends up doing everything at every turn because he or she feels that no one else is good enough.

**4. The very best boss you have ever had...ever.** This is the boss, the egotist, who can't accept that their employees have ever had a better boss, (could be a teacher or lover who feels the same). Their methods might be not so all-consuming as the stomper/gobbler, but the boss displaying this personality trait is still hard to live with and work for. They think they are the best and expect their employees to worship them.

**5. The Taskmaster.** Focusing only on the job, job, job. This is the boss who latches on and never lets go until employees are exhausted. Talk about leaving no one happy! Everyone in the office will be left thinking that all that matters is the bottom line. This person does not motivate—they *intimidate* to get tasks done the best they can be done. They're concerned only with maximum profit. Feelings be damned.

This is undoubtedly not the way I want my offices to be run or how I treat my staff. Yes, I am in the dental business to make money, but not at the expense of working my staff as if I don't care about them on a basic human level.

Have you heard the saying that people don't quit companies, they quit people? (I just love it when I can puke forth a platitude.) I believe this is true in a lot of cases in the workplace. Employees often leave because they are not being treated fairly by the people they work with, whether that person be coworker, manager, or especially, the boss. If the boss is any of the five types above or a combination of them, and devoid of emotional intelligence, then his or her attitude and actions might kill the spirit of an employee as much as influence the actions and mindset of his managers—who will then kill the spirit of the employees.

Of course, they might not be any of these five types. A bad boss might just be a natural a**hole.

## Climate Change

I have mentioned the word climate before. I am particularly proud of how I have attempted to continually address and regulate the climate in my offices to reflect the emotional intelligence by which I choose to live.

However, I will mention an example that happened well before I had ever heard the term emotional intelligence, so I have to pat myself on the back for being such a forward thinker or maybe I just saw a good way to avoid conflict. Either way, here's another example I used in my first book (if you can't steal from yourself, who can you steal from?) that illustrates what I knew to build, even though I didn't know what it was I was building.

There came a time in building my empire (empire with a little "e"), four years or so into owning my practice, when I opened my Dental Resource Management Group (DRMG). The plan was to have a central hub, where I could handle the day-to-day business of my practices. My accountant had been growing sick and tired of me dumping my mess of financial papers and scribbled receipts on his desk once a year, suggesting, at the very least that I get a part-time bookkeeper to keep my records in some basic order. But with my business growing so fast, that one hire turned into a whole staff. That staff needed a place to work, which led to me opening a separate office and company. I even toyed with the idea of training bookkeepers and hiring them out to other dentists to help those doctors sift through their financials.

Opening up this other part of my business worked well for all of us. It took a lot of the pressure of filing and keeping track of my financials off my back. It was great for my doctors and patients to have someplace they could go directly where these matters—billing, insurance, and various paperwork—could be addressed without getting those questions answered at one of my busy dental offices.

But the most critical factor that speaks to creating and maintaining a specific climate was that I had the common sense to integrate DRMG with the rest of my practices. As far as I was concerned, this was a support office not a corporate space. I would not tolerate an "us versus them" mentality between the practices and the management office. No attitude of doctors in one place butting heads with paper pushers in the other. In fact, the DRMG was across the parking lot from my busiest practice.

It was—and still is—up to me to create and consistently work at an atmosphere that keeps everyone feeling that we all work together. Regardless of their job, every one of my people is working for one company, under Dr. H. It doesn't matter which particular office you step into every day. It's still my office. I'm still the boss. I set the tone and create the atmosphere.

It was well worth the effort spent setting up and maintaining this climate.

# 11 The Emotionally Intelligent Way to Handle Criticism

The healthiest office climate in the world doesn't automatically yield smooth sailing for day-to-day issues. Any office has to deal with criticism. It doesn't matter who gives the critique or who receives it, emotional intelligence can offer guidelines for giving, receiving and digesting criticism. Criticism is a hot-button topic that we purveyors of emotional intelligence must navigate in an office environment. There is no getting around it. Like that couple who claim "oh, we never fight," be suspicious of the office where there is never any criticism.

But, I won't kid you, criticism sucks. Who wants to hear it? Who wants to be called out, dressed down, or told that they did something wrong?

It is essential then to learn how to deliver and accept criticism skillfully. Think of this in practical terms. Doing the work we do, aren't we forever being assessed, critiqued, and even second-guessed?

We invite it by so often asking our patients: "So, how do you feel?" "Are you in any pain?" Even the simple, "Can you bite down?" begs an answer. We can't do what we do if we don't know how to take and give criticism in a healthy, self-aware way.

## The One Critiquing

First and foremost, as the boss (teacher, leader, or manager), it is your responsibility to carefully consider your role in all aspects of your business. It is doubly so when you have to critique an employee. As the person who makes (or has the final say on) assessments, hands out assignments, and signs a paycheck, you hold a lofty position. If ever there are those occasions where it seems you are not being listened to, remember that what you say has weight. What you say, and how you say it, can really impact someone.

Use your emotional intelligence to say what you have to, in the best way you can. You want your words heard and digested, not merely considered a nuisance or, at worst, a real put-down. Remember, you are always erring on the side of nurturing good feelings, not bad. If the boss cares about others' reactions, empathy can make bad news more palatable.

You can't change how someone feels, but you can use EI to deliver criticism in a way that does not instantly prick someone's sensibilities or put them too quickly, and possibly permanently, on the defensive.

Often your point and what you are addressing is not what the person you are critiquing hears. There are many triggers and deep wounds the average person keeps right on the surface of the psyche. These wounds, worries, and anxieties often blister to the surface, even if the criticism being offered has nothing to do with that wound.

I have often felt that I was offering someone insight, only to discover they walked away wounded well beyond anything I could ever have imagined. Even if you don't mean to, hurting someone accomplishes nothing. And believe me, the whole office will know if and when criticism has been delivered well—and even faster if it has been poorly given.

*So how are we to avoid hurting someone?*

First and foremost, be succinct. Have a conversation in private and avoid the all-too-human tendency to paint with a broad brush. A statement like: "Every time you always do this..." is in direct contrast to what emotional intelligence teaches, which is to be direct, sympathetic, and specific. Also, this should not be an attack on the person, but merely addressing what they did.

In a word, focus! (Yes, you have heard me mention the "F-word" before.) This is also not the best time to make a sandwich. I'm not talking about having lunch. I mean that you should avoid that oft-used method of saying something positive, then slipping in the critique, then wrapping up with another positive quality. This makes you come across as sneaky.

Additionally, in using the critique sandwich, you traipse past one of the more essential parts of EI: being direct. If you have both positive and negative things to talk to a person about, do so at different times. Each delivered separately will have more of an impact and will not counteract the other.

Equally as important is to deal with issues when they occur. Resentment and ill feelings fester when someone holds off on telling another what they really felt in a situation or how they needed something done differently. Contrarily, if something is not addressed, the perpetrator can come away thinking they got away with it, or that their boss doesn't care about the quality of their work.

If you have ever trained a puppy, you know that if you do not address the wrong that they do the second they do it, they will not remember their offense if you wait and correct them later. I'm not equating people to man's best friend, but it is a good idea to follow this concept and address what's happening in a critical situation with co-workers, as well as family members, lovers, etc., as soon as it happens.

Remember, just because you want someone to listen to what you have to say and then have them change because of it, it doesn't mean they will. A supervisor delivering a less-than-exemplary annual review, or a comeuppance even, may assume that they have been heard, and that the critiqued employee will go away from the meeting ready to perform as they have been instructed.

But your criticism might not be implemented at all, or worse, the employee might not have even heard it in the manner in which it was intended. An employee who consistently opposes office policies or runs the risk of being fired acts as they do for a multitude of reasons. Your chastisement may, in fact, have no effect at all.

## The One Being Critiqued

It's not so easy to give oneself a pep talk after being criticized. As well-reasoned and warranted as the bad news may be, even a well-meaning "I just have to take that from where it comes" usually doesn't improve the emotional impact of receiving criticism.

The reality is that even constructive criticism can hurt. If you find yourself receiving criticism that impacts you more or harder than you expected, delve a little deeper into what you are hearing from your boss or teacher. Give yourself a little perspective, both yours and theirs, and consider just what it is about what they are saying and why it really bothers you.

Instead of taking a critique personally, think first: "What can I learn from what I am being told?"

Instead of focusing on the idea that you did something wrong, think about what how you can do it better the next time.

Suppose the criticism has really gotten to you. Your boss (or significant other?) leveled some sort of comment that hit a little too close to an insecurity. Before you get all red-faced over the critique and threaten to quit your job (or ask for a divorce?), think about what your critic was saying as opposed to what you think they were saying.

You may just be predisposed to take the hit in a certain way. Explore that wound. See if the critique has not, in some way, indirectly pricked an old worry. As you are developing your EI, use this as an opportunity to explore and consider what you can learn from this experience. Over time, your emotional responses will change, and you'll have the clarity to see the criticism for what it is and determine whether or not it applies.

In the end, the critique lands deeply because you allow it to. Whether constructive criticism, insults or a passing comment that you flick off your lapel, emotional intelligence gives you the strength to know how to take what you are being given.

Remember, there are two people in this equation. As much as the critic wishes to get a point across, as much as that critic wishes to be understood and heard, you can walk away with that criticism and go any which way you wish.

Another way to set a good defense against criticism is to look at what's being said from a mental distance. Set in your mind's eye to where you are and where your boss/teacher/parent is standing. Consider this as if you are watching a play of two characters interacting. This way you can regard your reaction while you notice the emotional state of the person delivering the criticism.

If you are emotionally aware, you will be clued into a wide range of insights, from what's being said and how it is being said to the body language of the speaker. Dealing with the moment in this way will allow you to think well, watch your every move, listen deeply, and consider your character's reaction.

As your boss or manager should, you also should keep this moment of criticism from your fellow workers. Nobody likes a crybaby, and everybody else has their own stuff to deal with. Maybe someone you usually run to was just criticized themselves last week. Good news or bad—what you are told about your performance or even about a possible promotion need not be shared.

If the person who criticized you did so publicly or runs out and shares their criticism with others, then shame on them! They are not very emotionally intelligent. In fact, this would be more of a reason to dismiss what they said to you.

All you can do is focus on how *you* act, so avoid looking for Karpman's rescuer or becoming a victim. It doesn't wear well, and you are missing the point about taking criticism tempered by your EI.

Lastly, no matter what was said, how much you will need to go back and redo or rethink, or how close you came to losing your job or spouse, *get on with getting on*.

Emotional intelligence teaches us to be present in the moments of our life, as much as to move ever forward from them. An inert psyche indeed gathers moss. We do no good wallowing. Licking your wounds brings about stewing, plotting revenge, and festering. None of these responses are the stuff of EI.

The thing to remember most, for both parties, is that there can be no progress without mistakes, and we all make them. I'd go so far as to say that without great big mistakes—which people indeed get criticized for, fired, and damned and chastised over—the most significant advances in society would not have ever been made.

# 12 Emotional Distance vs. Emotional Intelligence

In any form of medical work, we are taught that an emotional distance is needed so we can adequately do the very best for our patients. Inevitably, as dentists, we literally come into very close proximity to the folks we are attending. As medical professionals, there is still an unspoken strain of detachment that we—from heart surgeons to orthopedists, to dentists and endodontists— are taught to cultivate in order to do a good job.

But as far as I am concerned, skipping down the emotional intelligence side of the street, we can still do our job and muster the emotion a patient needs.

I have always believed that our procedures and schooling take care of themselves. Surely you have to go through it all. As a medical professional, you hit the books, cram the information between your ears, and then log the intern hours into honing craft and skill. As with most work, you get better the more you do that work. The doing of it reinforces the learning of it.

One of the hardest pieces of the puzzle to grasp, however, is cultivating caring and awareness of your patient's mental state, generally what used to be referred to as bedside manner. In all fairness, it's sometimes not so easy to build a warm and fuzzy relationship with people who we only see once every six months, and sometimes it's best not to engage while concentrating on working in their mouths.

Thankfully those old-school days of detachment are over.

And quite frankly, there were a lot of men and women in our field, as well as in other health care professions, who enjoyed the supposed rarified air they imagined they were breathing in their self-imposed, doctor-over-patient hierarchy.

You know the old joke: What's the difference between a surgeon and God? God doesn't think he's a surgeon.

It's nice to be the person with all the answers, who can significantly affect someone's life (or their chewing) and be highly-respected for one's skills and knowledge. Who wouldn't want that kind of reverence?

But being revered is not realistic and certainly not practical these days when, if anything, modern medicine seems to be moving more towards a doctor-patient partnership.

Really, how far can you hold your skills and knowledge from a patient these days? The average patient knows more about veneers than we do. They conduct all manner of research across the web and read countless reviews to find the best dentist for their needs. We had better come aboard to build better relationships rather than trying to keep one from forming.

In modern-day dentistry, we must err on the side of cultivating emotional intelligence in our practices because the modern patient expects it.

I know I'm throwing lots of stuff at you here. Most of it is theoretical, but the title and theme of this book is really about how dentists can apply emotional intelligence in dental offices.

These early chapters have talked a lot about personalities and some basic, everyday occurrences in our offices and in our interpersonal relationships. Now, we're going to dip deeper into the actual scenarios of the office. If you need an intermission, go make and butter your popcorn now.

Just be careful, you don't want to bite into one of those kernels and end up needing a dentist.

# SECTION TWO
## Implementing Emotional
## Intelligence Into Your Office

# 13 Emotional Intelligence and the Job Interview

I want to start this new section with that which I find myself doing, my managers undergoing, and the office consistently enduring: *The Interview.*

I can't speak for your practice, but between occasionally moving staff around, expanding practices and yes, sometimes people actually leaving the Shangri-La of working for me (can you believe it? People actually quit Dr. H.), we seem to be ever interviewing.

Through the years, my growing awareness and application of emotional intelligence in my practice has enabled me to learn what an interviewer should be asking, as well as what the interviewee should be answering, even when not requested.

I'm sure you've heard: "An ounce of prevention, is worth a pound of cure."

To this I add: "...and can lessen a ton of aggravation."

It takes time to incorporate even the best person into the right job. There are many obstacles both seasoned staff and a new hire will have to overcome, even when all the right pieces fit in all the right ways. Why set yourself up for failure from the outset? Make sure the interview is as informative and as informed as possible. Prevent and prepare yourself as best you can when bringing someone new into your practice, whether it's a receptionist or a new hygienist, by leading the interview with awareness.

**To the interviewee, I say:** answer questions and mock scenarios put to you with as much passion as you can muster. Give of yourself beyond what's asked. As someone who is constantly hiring people, I can tell you that what I want to see from potential employees is that they have the get-up-and-go—the awareness—for what's needed beyond the confines of the interview or even beyond what might be asked of them.

As my emotional intelligence has deepened over the years, my interviewing skills have grown by leaps and bounds. I have gotten better at placing the right person in the right position. I have avoided folks that, while qualified, lacked what I felt was needed for my particular practice. More often than not, what that person lacked was either a certain level of emotional intelligence or even the ability to be open to learning some. I have certainly made mistakes in my hires, as I have alluded to previously, but mostly I have made good decisions, as much from my smarts as from my senses.

As I have mentioned, I value EI as much, or even sometimes more, than IQ. A man or woman that has passed to the interview stage with us has to, at the very least, have the schooling, skill, and experience needed for the specific job we're looking to fill.

But beyond what's on their resume, I need to sense a basic level of humanity in a potential new hire. Anyone can learn the meat-and-taters of emotional intelligence while working for me, over time, but if you are not respectful of others, friendly—in a word, nice—I'm probably not going to hire you.

Of course, I understand that an interview can make anyone nervous, and I will cut everybody a break. I also expect to find a certain level of civility in potential employees, not the old chip-on-the-shoulder, "you'd-be-lucky-to-have-me-working-for-you-Dr.-H." attitude. Confidence is great, but not at the exclusion of decency. Without decency for your fellows, you can't grow emotional intelligence.

Being more in-tune with people and your environment, and humble when it comes to describing your good points and bad, can't hurt you with any potential employer. This is why the following five questions are so important to me when interviewing.

## Dr. H's Big Five Interview Questions

### Question 1: Tell Me About One of Your Worst Days at Work

**INTERVIEWER**: Just as this question leaves your mouth, you should lean in and assure your potential employee that you have bad days, too, maybe regale him or her with one of your own to put your interviewee at ease. You want to show empathy with emotionally-intelligent flavored questions, and not just be an observer. Impress upon your subject that you too have gone through the same things you are asking them to reveal.

Watch the interviewee as they begin to open up (or not) to your story. Observe their body language and breathing changes, as much as what and how they relate their own challenging example. If I had my druthers, I would ask the person facing me to describe one of the worst days of their life, but this might skirt the boundary of what is appropriate or what they feel comfortable sharing. Since this is all about what they might bring to my practice, keep this question work-related.

**INTERVIEWEE:** Be honest, dig deep, give forth a good one. This is not the time to cover up. Yes, you might appear vulnerable, but that's a good thing. The interviewer is not asking this just to make you feel uncomfortable. He or she really wants to know what you consider a bad day, *and how you surfed your way through it.*

## Question 2: What Can You Teach Me?

**INTERVIEWER:** I consider this more a softball question, opening a window into something the potential employee likes to do off the clock or as a side interest. It's quite interesting to see what the interviewee chooses to share, whether it is work-related or something from their personal life.

**INTERVIEWEE:** Here is an excellent chance to show the variety of your interests or impress upon the interviewer how passionate you are about something. Your potential new boss may also be looking to see what exactly you pick. Whatever it is, pick something that shows your passion and your personality.

## Question 3: Tell Me About a Time You Failed at Something and What You Did About It

**INTERVIEWER:** I find in this day and age that humbleness is a rare quality. Again, you can lead this to something that happened at your interviewee's work, but as you are trying to develop a bit of intimacy here, let your query dangle and have the interviewee give you an instance from whatever aspect of their life they want to tell you.

**INTERVIEWEE:** This is similar to question #1, but here you can really let loose with absolute abandon as well as show your mettle in how you rode the failure, picked yourself up, and came out of the circumstance a better person.

## Question 4: In What Way Are You Proactive or Disciplined?

**INTERVIEWER:** The answer to this can be very telling indeed. For instance, if you are a long-distance runner, and you respond that you run all the time, this is not exactly being proactive. But if you hate (and I mean HATE) running, but get up every morning to run before you shower so that you can drop those last 10 pounds, then you are being proactive.

**INTERVIEWEE:** When you need to go off script a bit, dig deep. Proactivity can come from many aspects of your life. Don't just use a standard line such as "I am a good worker and put my mind to any task no matter how hard it is." I *expect* that work ethic! Tell me something of how you apply yourself in a way that goes beyond a job or your usual comfort zone.

## Question 5: Describe an Ethical Dilemma You've Encountered at Work.

**INTERVIEWER:** Here you are getting into the gray areas and trying to learn about the make-up of the person you are considering hiring. Don't expect pat answers or even responses you agree with. Ethics, the very stuff of a person's moral make-up, is a deep, dark, and sticky place to toss and turn into. There are emotionally intelligent ways of dealing with conflict. What you want to determine is his or her belief system or world view.

**INTERVIEWEE:** This is an excellent opportunity to show how you work with others in the face of something that is challenging to you personally. We all know there are times when more than just the work gets in the way. The interviewer is looking to know the depths of you as a person and understand how you navigate sticky situations and problem solve.

***

Think of the interview process as a learning experience from both sides of the table: a real give-and-take and a substantial opportunity to come to some good old emotionally intelligent common ground.

# 14 Emotional Intelligence and Vulnerability in the Office

Interviewer and interviewee, boss and employee, student and teacher, surely two people in a romantic relationship...all need to allow some vulnerability to seep into their approach.

If you are constantly trying to appear as the all-knowing employee who never makes a mistake. Or if you play the omnipotent boss, you are going to fail. Trying to one-up a friend or worse yet, a spouse, at every turn, builds resentment. And believe me, your fall will be from a much greater height when you do eventually fail, as everyone surely does, if you set yourself up as the prince or princess of perfection.

Admitting your vulnerability, even if that vulnerability is a lack of knowledge and skills, shows that you are open to seek help and learn. And while I will admit that a boss, manager, teacher needs to maintain a level of decorum that befits his or her position, the more relatable they are—simply put, the more human a boss may seem—the more they will engender warm feelings from the people around them.

I know plenty of high-powered CEOs or crusty, old dentists say they'd rather be feared than liked. (How Machiavellian.)They believe that proficiency is born on the wings of people thinking their job is always on the line. But that's not the way I operate, and I genuinely believe it's counteractive to good emotional intelligence to instill a sense of shaky ground under people's feet.

But this is not all just on the boss or your mentor. On the flip side of the coin, employees, students and your spouse need to express their own vulnerabilities, too. It's just good EI to do so.

## When to Ask for Help

Let me give you an example of something that happened in our offices which emphasizes the importance of being able to admit ignorance and request help.

In need of a PowerPoint presentation, my managers and I sought help from an employee who we had just promoted. We thought he could do the job asked of him, but it turned out the individual wasn't comfortable using the program we needed him to use. Refusing to ask for assistance (I have to assume as the new hire he just felt it best to muscle through and not show weakness) and after a full month of fruitless back-and-forths well past the deadline, he finally delivered a report that was far below our expectations and did not address our needs.

Instead of reaching out and asking someone to show him how to use PowerPoint, our newly promoted employee delayed the work, made excuses, and had nothing useful to show for it in the end. How much faster and better for everyone would it have been for the individual to simply say, "I'm willing to help, but I've never used this program before. Could someone walk me through it first?"

Because of this person's fear of looking like a failure, the project stalled. But he should have asked for help. I have needed help plenty in my life. I understand when people need help, especially if they are being asked to do something with which they have no prior experience.

To my way of seeing things, part of working hard at a job—*and at life*—is to ask questions when you don't know how to do something. Allowing yourself to be vulnerable.

# 15 The New Associate Dilemma & Skewing Schema

In this vignette, I'm going to show you how schemas impact our very own data versus interpretation situations.

Occasionally, I meet with a group of fellow dentists who, like myself, have been running their practices for years. Whether they have one office or a few, we are all of a similar age, have been doing what we do for more than three decades, and seem to share the same war stories.

## The Texting and Social Media Generation

When we meet, we usually come around to complaining about the new associates we are hiring. It's not so much that we think their skills or schooling isn't up to par. It's that we see what we interpret to be a lack of sociability across the board. The kids coming out of college do not put themselves "out" the way we think new associates should. Certainly not the way we did when we were first hired.

Nobody goes around to referring dentists anymore, bringing bagels, introducing themselves and shaking hands. There is no one trying to round up an old school "lunch and learn." It seems to all of us that the new associates, the millennial dentists we are hiring, only want to come in, do the work, get their paycheck, and leave.

But my contemporaries and I had interpreted the data incorrectly. After talking the problem through (and damning a whole generation), we found we had more than a little bit of "oh those darn kids today" mass prejudice. We came to realize that dentists just getting out of college are, like us all, *products of their era*. The new dentists on the scene, almost all in their mid-to-late 20s, do not consider going around and shaking hands, simply because they do not do this in their personal life.

These millennial dentists grew up in a world of texting. They consider online or distance relationships just as legitimate as in-person, hand-to-hand relationships. How can you blame someone for different social behaviors when their learned habits are influenced by different cultural or generational norms? Self-awareness teaches us to consider not only someone's feelings, but also how they come to those feelings.

## Misfiring Schema

Sometimes, I encounter the very best examples of when emotional intelligence should be applied at other workplaces. The following example is a case of mistaken identity taken to its extreme. In this case, it was all a benign interpretation which began a chain reaction that never should have started.

I witnessed a customer in a store approach a woman that he had assumed was a clerk. She was dressed all in black, and wearing a vest, so it was a simple assumption. But the lady flipped out the second the "can you help me find..." was out of his mouth. I saw by the customer's reaction that he realized his mistake as soon as he made it, but it was all too late for apologies or even slinking away. The lady who had suffered the case of mistaken identity was in full-on blast mode.

What is the emotional-intelligence moral here for your office? Well, first and most obviously, to the person seemingly wronged: take it down a notch. Be aware that people can easily misinterpret information with no malice or prejudice.

Let me repeat this: *People make honest mistakes!* Man, if we'd all learn this lesson even a little bit, we'd save ourselves so many headaches. I truly believe that most people, especially your coworkers, are just trying to get through the day. They are usually not looking to lash out and hurt you deliberately.

Secondly, if something like this happens in your workplace, don't forget *you are in a professional setting*. Staff, and especially patients, do not want to see your explosion (or meltdown). Even if you have a legitimate reason to be hurt, taken aback, or full out 0-to-60 angry, keep yourself together while at your work.

Finally, for the person who makes a mistake, there is, unfortunately, no way of knowing from day to day what will set someone off and how big or small they might react. We try with EI to avoid our coworkers' triggers, but when faced with an emotional display, sometimes a quick apology and getting out of the way is the best course of action.

# 16 Emotional Intelligence as a Way to Read the Room

Across my many offices, the staff hold meetings about once-a-week. I attend some of them, while my team hosts others without me. In one meeting, our office manager invited someone from our marketing department to observe the roundtable weekly question-and-answer volley. The subject to be discussed had some relevancy to marketing, so she thought, why not?

I agreed to the invitation. The more the merrier in our meetings.

The problem was that the person invited in, who was supposed to act only as an observer, commandeered the meeting. She became the guest with a lot to say, and say it she did! I even saw my manager lean across the big round meeting table and give this pontificator the cut signal, swiping her finger across her neck. The invited lady just kept at it.

Of course, almost everybody in the meeting zoned out after a time. I never understand how those who drone on and on don't notice people starting to drool or nod out in front of them. And of course, the interloper played the victim when my manager later mentioned to her that her interfering was, well, interfering.

The lessons here? First, know your place. Use your emotional intelligence to sniff out your surroundings, especially when it is a situation that doesn't involve you but you might have been invited. Second, become as aware of other peoples' body language as possible. This sixth sense will pay you benefits in large group meetings or even sitting across the table from someone.

I instantly think of the line from that old Kenny Rogers song "The Gambler" in these instances: "You've got to know when to hold 'em / Know when to fold 'em / Know when to walk away / And know when to run."

Or simply, know when to shut up!

## Overstaying/Understaying Your Welcome

This next example happens all too often.

I really wish that the sales reps who come into my office would use a little extra awareness. You know how nutty our reception areas can get, how tense they can be. (Notice I didn't call it a waiting room. I like the sound of reception area better.)

All the latest magazines and friendly staff will not negate the fact that people are waiting. They are nervous and generally anticipating a dental procedure they really would rather not have. A sales rep walked into one of my practices the other day and, if it's even possible, made the reception area an even more uncomfortable place.

This day my reception area was pretty full. The place was buzzing. The phone was ringing off the hook. We were short-staffed that day. My receptionist was flying this way and that trying to make up the slack.

Into this mess, a sales rep came in to ply her wares, ignoring the mayhem and the crowd, plowing right ahead to my receptionist with her well-worn spiel. Now, I appreciate that she was looking to make a sale, it's her job after all, and the reason she came to visit my happy little hamlet. But maybe, just maybe, the lady should have had a look around and listened a little? I am sure, it would have seemed to even the most casual observer (emphasis here in the second word—one must be observing) that this particular day might not have been the best to give anyone on my office staff a sales pitch.

The salesperson in question stayed two hours, consistently pitching. We were getting complaints from staff and patients, and we all know, the very worst thing that can ever happen in an dental office is when patients start to get sick of hearing a sales rep.

The manager of the office had to actually walk the sales rep out, after she sat on our couch going on about why she was there. We actually sent an email to her company banning her and anyone from her company from returning. And really, this was the last thing we wanted to do. It's bad enough having to deal with these salespeople, let alone have to call their companies and complain!

I understand that being a salesperson is all about reaching projected goals, meeting quotas, and making sure you secure potential clients, if not an actual sale. It's a business based as much on popularity, and a good gift of gab, as it is trying to sell something to me that I might find useful. These people are in a pressure cooker to perform, but, there's a modicum of common sense and awareness that a salesperson, or anyone else in this situation, should have. A smattering of EI, a smidgen of self-awareness, a sniff of bustling air of one's environment, just stopping long enough to take the pulse of the room would have gone a long way.

Okay, enough about the bad behavior of others. It's time for me to own some stuff. In my case, it's often me under-staying my welcome.

As I have mentioned before, I suffer through typical self-induced ADHD. I am as much a victim as anybody to my chirping phone or a bright, shiny object catching my eye and sending me off on a tangent. One of my worst traits as a result of this is me constantly calling staff meetings at the last minute, with no real agenda in mind, or having an agenda that flies out of my mind by the time the meeting comes together. I often stop and start the hastily assembled get-together only to fly out of the room to answer my cell phone, leaving my staff sitting there, waiting for me to return. And when I do eventually come back, my train of thought has been so woefully derailed, I end up complaining that stuff isn't getting done, when I have yet to even address what that stuff is.

Then my cell phone goes off again.

In this case, I didn't stay long enough to overstay my welcome. I lacked the focus to do what needed to be done.

This is the thing with emotional intelligence: it only works when you use it. Whether you are the salesperson who everyone wishes would simply leave the busy office, or the boss who calls the meeting, but then jets out of the conference room door at every provocation, sometimes we spin our wheels and even though we are hoping for forward motion, we get nowhere...fast.

# 17 Emotional Intelligence Adds the Personal Touch

At this point, it should be apparent that lots of this stuff falls well across a few categories of emotional intelligence theory. Part of growing your EI is building your own insights to what you are experiencing. Your awareness should lead you to your conclusions, and which tools to use in a particular circumstance.

## Happy Birthday from Dr. H

Across my various practices and my Dental Resource Management Group, I have about one hundred people working for me. For most dentists that's a lot of employees, so yes, I am proud of what I have built. I am also proud that many of my employees have been with me a long time. I believe that this lack of turnover comes from my use of EI in the workplace and making the time to personalize my interactions with the staff.

One of the things I do is send out staff birthday cards. This is not a small detail, I assure you. It is something that speaks directly to the emotional intelligence that I try to infuse into my offices and my life. I have found that taking the time to mail (yes mail!) someone a card on their birthday, with a little personal note from me plus a Starbucks gift card, really goes a long way. As we all know ten bucks isn't about to buy very much at the local Starbucks, but my gesture is genuine and remembering someone's birthday means a lot. It means a lot to me when somebody remembers mine.

The way I see it, sending the card is a multilayered strategy. Here I am, the boss, taking the time to reach out to an employee I might not generally come into contact with, managing not just an acknowledgment of their special day, but including a personal message in the card. And it's an honest to goodness card, not one of those e-cards we know people send-off simply because their online calendar alerted them.

And really, who doesn't love getting something in the mail, even if it's just a lousy card from their boss and five-bucks toward coffee?

I'm not relating the above to pat myself on the back, nor do I want my employees to sit back with tears in their eyes, the open card dropped across their lap, marveling over what a great guy I am. I just like cultivating a healthy boss-employee relationships by weighing in on some's big day. My staff member might get a ton of cards or just a few, but I want to be in the mix, just to let them know that the head honcho where they work is sending his best greetings. It reminds them that I lead with my heart as well as my head in how I employ them, and that there is a human touch and warmth coming from the place where they spend a majority of their time.

Simply, I want them to know I care.

## Recognizing Life Events

Additionally, I try to send a card or leave someone a note when I notice something specific someone has done or to acknowledge an employee's significant life event. I see how hard people work for me, I know how important their paychecks are and how long it takes to save for a new truck.

Why not let someone know, at the very least by catching them as they pass by me at the office, "Hey, I saw your new truck, it's freaking great, lots of luck with that!"

See my point here?

From sending a card or a note, to stopping someone in the hallway at work to ask how they are, all of this is important and, furthermore, stuff I like to do.

## Bolstering those Work Relationships

Consider how hard it is to maintain a romantic relationship, and that's just two people trying to get along. Now consider how many people you can run into on a daily basis at your job, how closely you might come into contact with them and, in some cases, how vital they can be to you doing your job well. It's in your best interest to try and get along with your fellow co-workers. You really don't have a choice.

Sprinkle in the unique ingredient of working in a dental office, well, the speed bumps to interpersonal fun are limitless, no?

At every turn there are pitfalls and places where folks can get their feelings hurt. Signals can get crossed (the data vs. interpretation problem), and there are always plenty of areas where criticism is leveled, and taken the wrong way. We can't predict every one of our coworkers' moods or keep every single person's triggers in mind every single day, but we all can proceed with a caution and caring.

In the best scenario, we can use our emotional intelligence to help us mentor, build, and engender a lovely little family of folk who, although working most certainly for their weekly pay, could indeed come to like one another. At the very least, staff might be productive to the point that others find their productivity and civility comforting.

If you utilize EI to even a small degree and if patients can meet a friendly, happy staff who are civil to one another while walking between exam rooms and the waiting area, I guarantee the work culture will be better for your practice in ways you cannot even imagine.

# 18 Time Lock and Task Lock

Sure, I have a larger-than-usual dental practice, but I don't have a traditional human resources department. We have never rolled with giving out plaques for employee appreciation or full-on HR evaluations on performance. We come to assess our associates with more on-the-ground, what's-happening-in-the-office observations, that, with all humility, I feel I have set the ground rules for.

In order to accomplish all this feel-good, Kumbaya-singing boss-employee intimacy, I needed to create a *time lock* and a *task lock*.

What are these Steve, I hear you ask.

A *task lock* consists of disciplining yourself to get something done. Let's say, I have ten birthday cards or personal notes to fill out, and I know I am hopping on a two-hour flight. I set myself the task of getting everything written during the flight, which means I need to plan ahead, taking everything with me that I'll need so as to complete the task, including cards, gift cards, and the names and addresses of those on my list.

An example of a *time lock* could simply be setting aside an hour in the evening, after dinner and after the kids have done their homework, to make sure I spend time with all of my family in same room. I do not leave. I turn off the cell phone and concentrate on being aware and present with my loved ones for, at the very least, the prescribed hour.

A task lock and a time lock can overlap, but the important thing is that you set a goal for yourself. Marrying positive thoughts—ideas that you know will make the people around you smile, and assure them that they are cared for—is one of the results we should be hoping for when we apply emotional intelligence in time and task locks.

I also make time for meals with my staff. When I know a particular person is staying late or has had a killer hard week or even if the time is just right, I'll take everybody out to dinner or order in pizza at the very least.

When we do go out, I usually try to invite my staff's significant others. It's nice to acknowledge the life that people have beyond the office. Besides, I could be gaining myself an ally here. Those days my employee comes home from work disgruntled about their day or pissed at me for some reason, maybe their guy or girl will defend me.

"Ya know, Doctor H. seemed like a nice guy that night we went out with the office for pizza and beer."

That's the thing with a little extra care, it can extend beyond one employee or the entire office. Caring can impact someone's personal life outside their work. Emotional intelligence can send ripples for miles around across the stormy seas of someone's day.

# 19 Relieving Patient Emotions

Our patients are the bread-and-butter of our businesses, and as we grow in our EI, we come to understand that when emotions flare in them, as they often do, they flare for a multitude of reasons.

## Anxiety

Quite often in a work setting, and especially in a dental office where patients suffer genuine anxiety, it serves all of us—doctor, office manager, nurse, and receptionist—to find the source of our patient's emotion, and to utilize our skills to face what might be behind it.

I get it. I know doctors are rushed, juggling a handful of emergencies, and trying to get through the day, all while attending to the intricate work of delving deep into someone's mouth.

A dental office can surely be a chaotic place for the receptionist, too, trying to book appointments while simultaneously battling the waiting room and fending off sales reps. We all might think that we really don't have the time to attend to some patient fidgeting in the chair, but ignoring their obvious distress or placating them a simple "Mrs. Jones, I'm sorry you're feeling anxious today" won't help to alleviate, and will often exasperate, the problem.

Try and take the time, no matter who you are on the staff, to recognize when a patient is suffering through something, and address it if you can. If not, at least let their dentist know what you have observed.

We all know though, that mostly what patients feel with us, is anxiety. And luckily this can be addressed succinctly. The assistant attending the patient well before the doctor even sees them can offer, "We do these (fill in the name of the requisite procedure here) all the time" or "Don't worry, there's nothing to this, you'll be out of here in a jiffy."

Just a little extra attention, letting someone know that you acknowledge their worry, is enough sometimes to ease someone's stress.

## Anger

Anger, one of the bedrocks of ill-feelings, is something we do indeed see from time to time (from staff and patients both). Again, the reasons why some might be angry is multitudinous, it might not even have anything to do with what is happening around them at your office. But that rising-steam feeling is best defused as quickly as possible. Take the kettle off the boil!

By the time an angry patient sits down in your chair they have probably been rumbling for a while. Employ that EI and halt them off at the pass. The patient (or even a staff member) pulling their black cloud around the office suite is surely communicating that something is going on. There is a reason for all that huffing around the reception desk, being brusque and generally unpleasant. As much as you should question your nurse about why she's acting so grumpy, certainly put it to Mrs. Jones sitting back in your chair, "Tell me what's wrong, I want to help."

In the old days, dentists, doctors, and even Indian chiefs (ok, maybe not this last group) did not want to hear anything about what was on a patient's mind. If a nurse clued in her boss beforehand, it was met more with a "Hey, thanks for the head's up. I'll ask Mrs. Jones as little as possible" attitude.

But this hands-off approach serves nobody and it's not how I want anybody acting in any of my practices. I know patients will be out of the chair and the office soon enough, but don't simply be relieved to see somebody leave. Just as a patient surely should not walk out of a dental office with a procedure not done right, they should leave feeling better emotionally than when they walked in.

# SECTION THREE
# Implementing Emotional Intelligence at Home

# 20 Emotional Intelligence at Home ...Vulnerability

Even though this book is mainly about emotional intelligence in the dental office, I think it's essential to get directly into how it can come to bear on your home life, too.

I can understand why you might be reluctant to show your soft white under-belly at work, but at around people who love you, as I mentioned before, you should really allow yourself to be open, trusting, and vulnerable. Of course, not everyone has siblings, spouses, parents, or even kids that they can trust. If any of these are the case for you, I'm sorry.

I came from a home life that was quite supportive, although not precisely touchy-feely. My folks were not comfortable with outward displays of affection, but my brother and I were deeply loved by both my mom and dad. My parents were decent, hard-working, generous people, and my brother and I have remained still very close to this day.

For the sake of my examples, let's assume that you are not living a wildly dysfunctional home life existence. Every family is wacky in its own way, there's no getting around that. If it's a quirky, healthy wackiness, we'll be fine.

At home or in your family setting, the idea of showing more, or even some, vulnerability could easily come down to asking your children, spouse, or sibling: "What could I be doing better or more of, to be a better [insert family role], to you?"

Of course, by asking this question you might step right into one of those careful-what-you-wish-for scenarios. You might hear things you thought you wanted to know, but soon come to realize the answers are painful. But if you can allow this question to trickle out of your lips or even act in a manner that shows that you are open to change, you might be able to mend some fences and build better relationships. You could very well put the person you ask on notice to consider their place in the scheme of things.

In time your spouse, kids, or sibling might come to ask, "So, what could I be doing to be a better [relationship role] to *you*?"

# 21 | Data vs. Interpretation at Home

When it comes to data vs. interpretation, let me give you a recent example from a family vacation. You could also label this jumping to conclusions, but what follows is a perfect case of misinterpreting data in a personal situation.

Julie and I took the kids on a fantastic cruise with ports of call like Paris, London, and Dublin. It was a two-week whirlwind, a pre-back-to-school excursion for the whole family. Having amassed as much mileage as Julie and I have through executive/life-coaching, and running across the world for my son's hockey tournaments, we managed to secure first-class seating for the whole family which made flying from Arizona to Paris much more enjoyable.

One of the many perks of first class is that even before the plane's main cabin door shuts, flight attendants walk down the aisles asking passengers what they would like to drink. Julie and I were asked if we would like a glass of champagne. I'm not a big drinker, but this was the start of our vacation, the booze was free, and I figured we could sit back, toast the trip, and chill.

My biggest goal for this vacation was for it to be a nice, relaxing trip. However, as you may have realized by now, it's hard for me to turn off. I often find myself traveling to some new place for a seminar, running in to cover for an endodontist who might be out for a week, or working to get our coaching and leadership business off the ground. Even when I am relaxing, the cell phone is going off constantly, and my brain is usually split between a few dozen things I need to do.

Added to my innate, more-than-slightly wild energy for this trip was knowing that we would be navigating our family through big European cities. Even in the best of scenarios, this trip could be challenging. It was certainly something I was looking forward to, but there was potential for a few obstacles along the way. My awareness was set on high, my internal monologue repeating, "Steve, don't sweat the small stuff" mantra-like in my mind.

My goal was to keep the kids happy and Julie on the same page with me as much as possible (or me on hers) in order to make this a great time for everybody.

But when Julie refused the champagne, opting instead for a glass of water alongside my drink, I got frustrated.

Why? Oh, who knows!

It just irked me that there we were, starting this trip, that I was going to do my best to make this a wonderful adventure, quiet my usual kinetics, and my wife couldn't just have a flute of overpriced (though it was free) bubbly with me.

By the time we were in the air though, I had let it go. We settled into the long flight, and I figured the "Julie-refuses-champagne" moment was just a blip on the radar. Still, it had blipped, I got some data and interpreted it, not even thinking that I might have interpreted wrong.

The moment passed.

We land and negotiate Paris with the kids in tow; and I have to say, my kids were great! They seem to be learning this emotional intelligence stuff from dear old dad. (God, I only wish it was from me!) We made the most of three full days in that big city and then headed for the boat to start our cruise. We boarded, and what do Julie and I find in our room?

A complimentary bucket of ice with a bottle of champagne chilling in its center.

As you have read: I'm not a big drinker, but this was the start of our almost two weeks on the boat, the booze was free, and I figured my wife and I could sit back, toast the trip and chill.

Sound familiar?

"Let's have a drink," I said to Julie, plucking the bottle from the ice like King Arthur and his sword from the stone.

"Nah, that's okay," Julie said.

Here was more data and, of course, more interpretation from it (none of it good), with me saying to myself, "Ok, here we go," in as flippant an internal monologue as I could manage without grumbling out loud.

Really disappointed, my EI like Elvis up and leaving the building (or jumping ship). I tried my best not to show that Julie's refusal of a second drink now, with me, her one-and-only present husband, on this, our wonderful vacation, was really bugging me!

We go on with the day. I might have been boiling inside, but I did my best not to ruin anybody else's time with my bad feelings about Julie not drinking with me a second time. Being a sensitive guy, things like this bug me and I admit, although I tried not to, I was waddling along all day in my negative interpretation of events.

It was later revealed to me that everyone noticed that I was muted, a little off my game.

I guess I don't hide it as well as I think I do! Then again, most of us don't hide things well, do we?

When Julie and I got around to talking about my apparent off mood, what had set me off, and what I felt with her refusing the champagne (twice), really meant to me, she matter-of-factly reminded me of one little fact.

"Steve, I hate the taste of champagne."

Someplace in the back of my mind I knew this, of course, but when your feelings get hurt you tend to ignore the little details. This had clearly been one of those instances where I was blinded by my own flipped trigger. I let go all logic and pulled myself full fetal into "No, this is my ball, you can't play" as the hurt set in.

"Now, if you were to go get some coconut rum and pineapple juice," my wife added with her killer smile, "I'd probably knock back two or three of those with you."

It wasn't that my wife didn't want to sit and have a drink with me! I had known all these facts about her dislike of champagne and her preferences, but I was too into feeling sorry for myself to factor in that it was that I who had misinterpreted data.

All I had to do was:

🕉 check my feelings and why I was having them,

🕉 dig down a little deeper and realize that Julie doesn't roll passive-aggressively, so that

🕉 her refusal of the champagne had to be something benign, and

🕉 recognize that even with an evolved sense of emotional intelligence, anybody can get waylaid by jumping to conclusions and interpreting data incorrectly.

## One Month Later: More Relationship EI

Julie and I celebrated our anniversary by going out to a nice romantic dinner. The evening was going great. I had enough sense to leave my phone in my pocket. I had made a vow not to excuse myself for a supposed bathroom break to check my messages. (Do you do that, too?) When we sat down, the waiter offered us free sparkling wine.

I said yes, but quickly checked the drink menu, found what was called a "Planter's Punch" rum drink and asked Julie if she wanted one. She hit me with an enthusiastic yes, and we were on our way.

It was a great dinner.

The only hiccup came when we stepped outside to the valet. As I attempted to negotiate the tip, thinking ahead as I was to maneuver around the busy valet station, I hurried to the driver's side door when the car came. Julie opened her door and got into the passenger seat.

"Ya' know, no big deal," she said as we drove away, "But it would have been nice if you had gotten the door for me."

In this instance, my wife extended her emotional intelligence, did not get mired in data vs. interpretation (why I didn't open her door). She merely told me her reaction and left it at that. No further stewing or bad feelings came. You've probably already guessed who is the more emotionally intelligent of the two of us, huh? Julie got it right.

We all get our feelings slightly nicked from time to time by people who really would never want to hurt us. It's human nature to make these unknowing slip-ups. We need to use our EI or simply a little extra awareness from time to time to focus on that which matters, and not sweat the small stuff.

# 22 Emotionally Intelligent Communication

This next story goes back to my dating days. I'm not so much pining for a younger care-free time where my responsibilities were nil (ok, maybe it's a little bit of that), as I am tip-toeing through the tulips of my past, where I often realize that I wasn't all that emotionally intelligent as a younger man.

## Say It Out Loud

One evening I went to pick up my date, and although I thought "Wow, she looks really fantastic tonight. The hair, the clothes, the makeup, wow!" I did not tell her what I was thinking.

Why? I have no clue.

But as I drove to the restaurant, and we sat across from one another over our meals, my date understandably grew a good head of steam over the fact that I had not said a word about how she looked. (I'd later learn it took her three hours to prepare.) She interpreted the data of my not speaking as me not noticing, not caring, or the worst scenario, that I didn't think she looked all that good. In a rare case of me not saying anything, I had said volumes, or so she had interpreted and then assumed.

I'm sorry to say this was probably one of many times I did not give forth on what I was feeling, but should have, where a lady was involved. I think I have since learned, but I'll have to check with Julie to make sure.

What I did not know on this date decades ago is that people have needs they often can't, or think they should not have to, express. I bring this up because, even though I know I have grown by leaps and bounds, it bears repeating that part of growing EI is caring enough to pay attention.

## Keep It to Yourself

As I mentioned before, I am pretty suspicious of those couples that claim that they never fight. I am equally suspicious of those who claim they tell each other everything. Sometimes there is nothing to be gained by revealing some fact, past occurrence, or even current dilemma, especially if doing so will exhaust or aggravate someone.

Please have the emotional intelligence to keep your mouth shut!

I simply am not equipped to tell Julie everything. Why? It's less my failing memory as it is that I know she doesn't want to hear it all. Why would she? We are mature enough, and have been married long enough, to realize what is important, what should be discussed, and what shouldn't. But I am not going out of my way to keep anything from my wife.

Unlike most couples, we work together, so we usually know what's going on a little too much in one another's existence anyway.

Really, does she need to be let in on every snippet of minutiae I am experiencing, or do I need to know all of the flotsam and jetsam of her day? I like to think I am there for her, as she is for me, to let her air the good and the bad, the trivial and the monumental, but part of this emotional intelligence stuff is getting to know what is substantive and what is not.

Time for another joke: Did you hear about the couple who were married for 50 years?

The secret to them staying together for so long was that there was nothing they wouldn't do for each other...so that's exactly what they did, they went through their 50 years doing nothing for each other.

Of course, you can't work through these nondisclosure moments with anyone if your relationship isn't strong. There must be trust. But there are just times when even I get sick of hearing myself talk, and Julie feels the same way about my babbling. Just because something happened in my day and Julie is my wife, need I reveal something I know she is not interested in?

Let me give you a hypothetical scenario.

You run into an old girlfriend or boyfriend down at the mall. This is someone you are on good terms with and haven't seen in a bit, but they are also the person you dated hot and heavy before you met your wife or husband. You and the ex share a few minutes catching up, flick through the requisite baby pictures on your respective phones, then part after ten minutes with a quick hug and a "have a nice life."

The moment is over and done.

Now say this person is, for whatever reason, a thorn in the side of your spouse. You have never given your wife or husband a reason to be jealous, and the ex is from way back in your past, but for some reason, your spouse doesn't like him or her.

So then, in a full-disclosure, got-to-tell-the-spouse-everything scenario, you spill the beans over who you met at the mall and spend the rest of the evening assuring them that they have nothing to worry about, or worse, getting the cold shoulder treatment for doing nothing more than talking about your kids with an old friend.

People share tidbits like this, even unduly poke and prod each other, all the time. Come on, you know they do. I could go into yards and yards of text here about how the more emotional intelligence we have, the less we will be jealous, but that's a load of crap.

We are humans. Stuff gets under our skin. At times, we like to see how much somebody cares for us by throwing some itching powder into somebody's day. We all go for the jugular sometimes for a variety of reasons, the most insidious reason: to tweak the other person. Sometimes, we simply are careless.

Dare I say, if you have a modicum of smarts and a good smattering of emotional intelligence, you will avoid full disclosure, for the multitude of reasons I give above, when what you might disclosure matters not a whit.

## Shut Up and Listen

In attempting to do anything I can to make my wife and kids' lives as easy and worry-free as possible, I tend to act on the "okay, if you have a problem, tell me about, and I will fix it" principle.

Of course, there are plenty of roadblocks that come up in any of our lives that can't really be fixed. Sometimes we just need to let off a little steam over our frustrations. And in building my emotional intelligence I have come to realize that sometimes all any of us want is to be heard. All we need sometimes is someone to scream at or two ears to bitch to.

More often than not we aren't even looking for a solution or an agreement. We just want to know someone we love is listening. I consistently have had to quiet that I-need-to-make-everything-right superpower I imagine I have and merely sit across from Julie or one of my kids and let them vent.

I find this is more frequently applicable for my very personal relationships. This makes sense because your spouse, kids, parents, or siblings are more likely to come to you with something more intimate than anyone you work with or employ. The key is that no matter who comes to you, or why, let them unburden unencumbered.

## To Advise or Not to Advise?

That is the question.

Unless a family member or close friend is particularly asking for your advice, just listen, hold a hand, let the person cry on your shoulder, and don't say anything.

I know this is hard to do. Especially if you, like me, love to offer a seemingly viable solutions but stop yourself from jumping feet first with that solution.

The very best you can do is to let the person telling you their tale of woe or their latest frustration know that you are listening. The last thing they want is to be placated. This translates into you "yes-ing" someone to death.

It doesn't matter the age of the person who needs your ears. We all have these moments when we are feeling down and out, done in, frustrated, unappreciated, or totally undone. I have witnessed a six-year-old child spin out of control while trying to articulate a frustration, just as I have seen adults completely unravel, beaten down by their day.

Trying to make sense in the face of our all-too-human meltdowns or an emotional surrender is a fool's errand. There will be time for applying logic or for considered solutions and calm, rational thought later. First and foremost, as an emotionally intelligent sounding board, calm the storm by being the safe port in it.

As someone with a good handle on your emotional intelligence, you should be all too aware that the giving of an opinion, even if asked for, can lead to less-than-favorable results. As the listener, if you come to an opposite conclusion to the problem presented, you might see an instant shut down from the person you are trying to help or work your way into an argument. Or, as so often happens when you give advice, it's even agreed with, but what you most end up doing is just fueling the fire of a tirade.

There can also be occasions where the person who has unloaded on you is looking for an argument, as much to release steam as to hear out loud their reasoned point of view. Again, this is all best avoided by begging off giving advice, even if asked for it.

Leading with the unspoken attitude of "just tell me what it is, lay it out, and we can deal with trying to solve it later" is always better than looking to impart advice, which can often become the classic "damned if you do, damned if you don't" scenario.

Even if you have a difference of opinion, who cares at this juncture? Contrarily you don't want to be accused of placating. As I suggested earlier, be like Switzerland. Stay neutral, stay quiet, and lend an ear. In the instance of being there for someone, just be there...but please, be quiet.

# 23 Emotional Intelligence and Children

I don't think there has been ample scientific study yet made to measure when a child should be growing emotional intelligence, but I can still advise on how to use (or not use) EI with kids. We certainly know that little brains take a while to develop, and do so in amazing stages.

Babies go from one day speaking gibberish to suddenly saying whole words. It's a wonderful unpredictable process to watch. I have multiple children and observing each one's mental development has amazed me as much as watching their growing physical abilities.

Your emotional intelligence can be put to substantive use when trying to help a child through a crisis, avoid their triggers, and most of all, empathize. Little feelings can get hurt mighty quick in that big, bad world out there, and sometimes a brief explanation that what happened wasn't directly meant to hurt your child or to illustrate the sad fact that their friends can sometimes be insensitive, are good talks to have.

With children, I believe that there are times when it is useful also not to apply emotional intelligence. I have found there have been equal times that not interjecting any opinion or even sympathy is often the way to go.

"Work it out amongst yourselves" is a phrase I have used all too often where my kids are concerned, and I have equally heard it said amongst my friends when speaking to their battling little ones. Interceding with a reasoned, calm overview, getting to the heart of everyone's motivations, and airing the entire episode are techniques that work great with adults, but not always so well with children.

Little brains are often not ready to grasp the tenets of awareness. Many times, all a child wants when they skin their knee is to be held and comforted. Come to think of it, this response is the only one we sometimes want as adults as well.

My point is, while there are times to engage your emotional intelligence with your kids, choosing not to is a better option much more frequently.

As with most things, emotional intelligence should start in the home. Our homes are ground zero for establishing the most intimate relationships we will ever come to know, and both children and adults will benefit from learning what to do or not to do in any given situation by what they are taught or see in their day to day familial interaction. This is why so any of our traumas are rooted way back from childhood, the stuff we experience growing up can cut deep furrows.

I'd like to think we are all budding little EI-ers, on our way to an enlightened state of awareness, but I know many people never see a hint of emotional intelligence in their homes. I wish more people did.

The three big negatives that can come from what we learn in our homes that thwart EI growth are:

ᚻ families who ignore one another,

ᚻ families who give only the most cursory attention to one other,

ᚻ and families who are out-and-out contemptuous of one another.

I hate to think about it, but I know there many families who never even get a whiff of all the good I've been talking about in this book, and will go on to perpetuate negative habits into the extended families of their workplace or to the kids they have down the line.

It really behooves you to try and apply E.I. with those you are closest to, those who know you the best and see you at your worst. Cultivating a habit of viewing and responding to situations with even the smallest amount of awareness and empathy (as well as knowing when to step back and not intercede) will soon transfer over to those you work with and serve.

# 24 Emotional Intelligence and Social Media

In the introduction of this book, I noted that Dr. Dan Goleman's listed social skills among his four parts of emotional intelligence. If the good doctor is correct, man, are we ever in trouble these days!

I would be the first to defend progress. How could anybody who works in our field not be thrilled by the advances we've seen in the past few years? Computer imaging, lasers, and ever-better compounds for molds and filling! It has been a whirlwind for us just trying to keep up.

But keep up we do, providing better comfort to our patients, and more efficient work methodologies in our offices.

Of course, there is a downside to all this progress. We don't get the good without the bad.

Because of the convenience of getting what we want almost before we know we want it, we are happy to rationalize the negative aspects of our technology. It's easy to convince ourselves that there is nothing bad about technological advances, which isn't the case and cannot realistically be.

If you don't see how the digital age—tweeting, texting, downloading, posting—is a direct detriment to emotional intelligence, then put down your cell phone and let me enlighten you.

## It Just Ain't Real

We tend to think that since we can communicate with people from half a world away, we are building relationships. However, these modes of communication, speedy and seemingly far-reaching as they are, actually keep us from coming closer to people. A relationship or reactions between two people that relies mostly on digital interaction—whether through text, Snapchat, or Instagram—does not foster the warmth and empathy a face-to-face encounter can.

I know it goes against the grain of the millennial paradigm, but texting someone instead of calling them; preferring a Skype, Zoom or Teams meeting over brainstorming with your peers in a conference room; or posting your latest vacation adventure on Facebook is not intimacy.

It's not even all that interesting. Even if you ignore what I am saying, even if you are feeding into the problem, you can certainly see the detachment that has come from all of this, can't you?

Many people thrive on that detachment, but if anything is an anathema to emotional intelligence, this new way of communicating with one another is.

How close are we, really, when we are using our cell phones less-and-less to make actual calls, and more to text and post or read comments? What kind of real communication are we having when language is beaten and battered down to emojis? Grab a table at any busy restaurant and watch partners or even whole families sit around the table, nobody once looking up from cell phones during the entire meal.

I postulate, from my old fuddy-duddy perspective, that what we have wrought with our current social connecting is so pervasive, satiates us on such a primal level, has so insidiously rotted our ability at civility and truncated our moments of humanity that we have come to not know any better…or worse, that we are growing not to care.

### An Itchy Twitter Finger Won't Get You Any Friends

If you live a life where you can, and do, blast every utterance to the masses (as the masses wait for the chance to do the same at you), you begin to believe that every morsel of your opinion matters. That posting on Instagram is important. That racing home to sully forth a Yelp review has some real value.

We already went over how social media breeds the passive-aggressive, but even for those of us without a specific motivation to get back at somebody, interacting with the world by not really interacting with it causes us to lose sight of the stuff that maybe, just maybe, we should take a breath and temper ourselves from saying.

You can't tell me you haven't noticed simple civility dying off this past decade.

Can you honestly report that there has never been a time that you've texted something that you came to regret the minute you hit your phone's send button?

Just because *you can* doesn't *mean you should.*

Every one of us shows our *vulnerability*. We see it in our frightened patients as much as we see it when a member of the staff is having a bad day. Using adequately developed emotional intelligence, and a little application of awareness, you should know what to say to someone who is hurting or displaying some stress, as well as when not to mention a thing to them.

But social media has rubbed our social filters down to tissue paper. I'm afraid too many of us don't know what to say when facing someone (and I mostly mean patients in this context) having a moment. We are so usually distanced from face-to-face interaction we simply do not know how to act or react with our fellow humans.

Yes, we damn well need E.I, now, *more than ever before*, because being 'on' as much as we all are, simply bleeds the humanity from us.

Emotional intelligence should teach you to recognize the why, what, and when of a situation and how to best to react to it (again, I mostly mean patients in this context). You should learn to consider feelings and not rush to judgment. In a society where we think we are multitasking with ever better skill, what we fail to see is how much we are missing or how ill-equipped we tend to be when it comes to that which is essential.

Sorry, but none of us is doing all that great a job out there being nice, or even civil, to our fellow humans.

## The Big Three

We've also forgotten the *Golden Rule* of polite conversation, at least the Golden Rule as I learned it. I grew up in a time when people did not discuss certain subjects in public.

*The Big Three* things that never belong in polite, public conversations are:

- religion
- politics
- sex.

These days, because we are "talking" so much all the time, to countless others who are talking right back at us ("at" or "to," but never "with"), we seem to think that those three no-no subjects, and a whole lot more, are fair game for any conversation, tweet, or text. Losing this ability to know what should and should not be aired, whether it's our own business or exposing someone else's business, affects how we measure and meter what we should and should not say, how we should or should not say it, and mainly, how we come to care for others

## No, Your Smart Phone Isn't Making You Smarter

Look, I don't want to get off on a rant here, as Dennis Miller used to say, but this stuff is dangerous.

The way I see it, smart phone technology has created a massive roadblock to the better building of emotional intelligence. The second word in our favorite phrase here is intelligence, and we need to cultivate ours while we come to understand, use, and marshal our emotions.

If you are not feeding your brain with experience (and no, Snapchatting is not an experience), you are doing yourself a disservice. Read a book to imagine scenarios, characters, and concepts in your mind's eye. Debate with colleagues or friends (without picking up your phone to check facts). Even indulge in a game of checkers every now and again.

If you do not use that gray matter up there in your noodle, your brain is going to atrophy, just like any other muscle will if not regularly used. It's a sure case of "if you don't use it you lose it," and we see folks losing it on a daily basis, unaware of how brain lazy they are becoming. I am sure you have noticed how predictive text programs (AI in action, folks) now provide us with possible replies even before we start typing anything. Talk about not thinking for ourselves any longer!

There is also the matter of being given too many options, fashioning the world around us to a well-appointed Netflix/Hulu queue or letting Pandora/Spotify suggest tunes.

Where is the learning in that? Gone are the days when we stumbled across a new author through good old-fashioned research or learned something new, simply for the sake of gaining knowledge.

When you are immediately given choices from an algorithm that has seemingly figured you out because of your clicks and search preferences, you limit yourself to the same old routine because said algorithm comes across a few of your Facebook friend's feeds. Ironically, in this world of seemingly limitless supply, we don't really travel so far afield. The modern brain only stretches as far as the vessel that contains us...or in the case of our digital word, that which satiates us.

# 25 Forgoing the Digital for the Personal

When you use texting and other forms of social media as your sole form of communication with your friends and family, you could come to the conclusion that since you already put it (whatever it is) out there, there's no need to communicate personally with anyone.

This is an insidious habit and something I see played out constantly. It can erode any progress we make towards emotional intelligence, because we can become lazy from what social media engenders.

It strikes me as ironic that in this day and age, where we can get and keep in touch better and faster than any time before in history, there are so many instances where I am not getting a call back or an email returned. Of course, when this happens in my personal or professional life, I tend to chase somebody down for a response.

After evolving from a working endodontist with several practices to authoring books, and now devoting my time to executive/life coaching, I cannot be so lazy in my relationships. I cannot play a passive role. It is my job as a coach to keep on the person I'm coaching, hopefully leading by example that being proactive is how one gets more from life.

How could a coach be anything less than the most proactive person you meet?

Emotional intelligence flourishes in an active state, in confronting, being ever aware, and challenging yourself and others. But plenty of people think that since they have tweeted their latest bit of news or that they are "on" all day, they are communicating in some substantive way.

Why ever should they email or call you back?

It seems that "common decency" is no longer as common it once was.

## A False Sense of Accountability

Maybe having a GPS tracker on your teenager is a good idea, but I see adults all the time thinking that they have to account for where they are and how long they might be there.

How often have you left a message with someone, only to have them call you back, and the first morsel they offer you is where they were and why they couldn't get to your phone call? Or how about how crazy we get when we shoot a text to someone and don't get a response within minutes?

This is beyond mere impatience.

This shows a lack of emotional intelligence on the most basic of levels. Rather than assuming that someone has a good reason for not getting back to us immediately, we jump to the conclusion that our time is more important than theirs and take offense that we are not priority #1. The reality is they could be driving, in a meeting, in the middle of an important conversation, or, if this is even possible, they didn't have their phone with them.

Welcome to the new, self-centered norm.

This norm is not so healthy.

We like speed. We are lazy and will always choose convenience over quality. Being able to get information and keep connected satiates us in a way we haven't formerly experienced. There seems to be something about our cell phone text alert that tickles our reptilian brain, like nothing else in modern society has ever been able to. Being distracted consistently from our lives, our family, friends, or jobs on any substantive level really doesn't do us any good. We all need to take time for quiet moments and settling our minds.

Sure, there might very well be a great big conversation going on out there. So what?

You are not feeding your brain by continuously catching and reacting to every little thing (an impossible task anyway). Maybe the search makes us feel like we belong or have our finger on the pulse of the latest news and gossip. We want to be in the know and flaunt our so-called knowledge to those who are not.

I have lived long enough to remember a time before cell phones and being constantly connected and there is a delineated difference between that then and this now. These days it seems that we're too busy Instagramming our selfies and growing our following to actually talk to the people in the background of our pictures and lives.

# 26 Emotional Intelligence, Sex and Gender

W hat are the specific differences in male and female emotional intelligence, if indeed there are any, and how do they play out in the workplace? Does that old male/female "Mars or Venus" conundrum rear its head when we consider emotional intelligence?

Most psychologists state that EI is the same, irrespective of gender. Like Kevin Costner in *Field of Dreams*, maybe if you build emotional intelligence it will come, whether you're a guy or a gal.

But there are ways men and women use their awareness differently, and biological determinants as well as cultural indoctrination come to cause this difference. Note here that I make my observations from the basis of being a heterosexual male in my mid-50s. I can't assess the world around me in any other way, so take what I say from that perspective.

Since it's considered a softer skill, dealing with feelings and all that folderol, women in our culture are expected to be more emotionally aware than men. Even with modern female empowerment making monumental strides in the workforce, mixing and matching emotion with thought is generally seen as something the fairer sex can and does do better. Surely lots of ladies have been hindered in the workforce by this assumption.

"How can she be a good boss or leader when she is obviously more prone to emotion?"

And yet we know, and have demonstrated throughout the book, that emotion is a positive aspect of being a leader and in being a better person in general. It must enter into the equation for someone to work at peak efficiency. Too much of the popular definition of leadership is based on aggression, which is generally something little boys learn or are prompted to acquire through their sports and play, more so than little girls. In my childhood the lines were clearly defined. Boys played War, and girls played House.

There are exceptions, but even today, a young girl is labeled a tomboy when she shows more of a leaning towards aggressive schoolyard competition than for playing with dolls. In the cut-throat business world, if a woman "acts like a man," she can be called much worse.

We are making strides to beat back a lot of these older modes of pigeonhol-ing the genders (sometimes in good ways, sometimes so zealously we miss the mark) but we all know that stereotypes still exist.

It has also been suggested that women have a more innate sense to influence, where again, men are more aggressive when put into leadership positions. We know influence is one of the better offshoots of emotional intelligence and is undoubtedly easier for co-workers to swallow than browbeating.

It also might be true that women develop better emotional intelligence in the workplace, and more of it, than men, simply because they have had to. Necessity might indeed have been the mother of EI invention, as women have had to hone a wide variety of skills, having faced more barriers than men when climbing the corporate ladder.

Then there is the consideration of how the male and female brain are dif-ferent. There seems to be a real difference between how men react, as opposed to how women react, especially when it comes to problem-solving and the application of empathy.

There are exceptions, of course, but when women are faced with a circum-stance where they have to be empathic, they tend to stay tuned in for longer than their male counterparts. Men, on the other hand, tend to jump past the emotion to get to the problem-solving. This is one of the precise differences the famous Mars versus Venus book[17] illustrates, and one where most people who study this kind of stuff (both men and women) agree.

Women might be better equipped to give and receive feedback (criticism, that we covered previously), where men tend to puff themselves up and take a stance against negatives coming their way. Although again, this sticking-to-the-feeling-of-things longer could make women more prone to gossip (or listening to it) than men. Still, I know plenty of men who are the source of office gossip.

Having worked with plenty of women in my life and most importantly, working alongside and building a business with my wife, I have firsthand knowledge of how a man (me in this case) and a woman (Julie) handle work.

By no means can I report that things have always been one hundred per-cent rainbows and roses between Julie and I as we have worked in our dental practices, while building Dental Resource Management Group or now, in growing our executive coaching/leadership company. I find that when we butt heads, it's as much because I'm a guy and she a gal, as it is that we are just two different people, headstrong and smart with firm and fast opinions. As we seem to do at home, we compromise as much as we dig in our heels, are empathetic as much as we are obtuse, and are steadfast as much as we are vulnerable, pretty much in equal measure.

I value Julie's opinion. Some of this value comes from the fact that she is my wife. I know she always has my back and always wants what's best for our lives and the business. She is very intelligent, and a trained therapist, so she has a

---

17 *Men are From Mars, Women are From Venus,* John Gray, Ph.D.
https://www.amazon.com/Men-Mars-Women-Venus-Understanding/dp/0060574216

lot of understanding of people and motivations. Julie has built our businesses and our life equally with me and has an equal say in what we do and how we do it. I also know that Julie is emotionally intelligent.

I believe that men and women have their strengths and weakness, as much because of their different chromosomes as because all people are different from one another. As people, we change constantly from a variety of factors and influences.

Regardless of any differences, emotional intelligence serves both sexes well.

# 27 The Dirty Words of Emotional Intelligence

When it comes to emotionally intelligent communication, heck, all communication really, the power of words is so very important. What we say and how we say it, as well as how we define our own or someone else's actions, will set the tone for our mindset. We will either have others lining up to join us on the Yellow Brick Road to Oz or conversely steering away from us post-haste. I'm sure you have seen both negative and positive effects of one word or phrase you've used with a loved one or a co-worker. It's bad enough that we reuse terms and definitions in our own lives that over time will keep us stuck, but we may be completely unaware of the effects those same words have on our friends and family.

I think of the infamous George Carlin classic comedy skit, "Seven Words You Can Never Say on Television."[18] (If you want a good laugh, search for it on YouTube.) Taking off from Carlin, I believe we need to avoid saying certain words and phrases if we're going to approach people with a more enlightened and evolved emotionally intelligent mindset.

Don't misunderstand me. I am not advocating for the overt political correctness of current society where we worry over every utterance. That kind of overly sensitive self-censorship is just as dangerous as being none too self-aware. I just think that we need to be aware of what we say and how we say it and if possible, avoid hitting below the belt or saying stuff we will regret later.

Trying to be more aware of our words might also slow us down some, which is actually a good idea when interacting with someone. If you find yourself itching to say something or a quick caustic phrase is just aching to get out, err on the side of avoidance or, at least, reprhasing.

The following list contains words or phrases you should just steer clear of entirely.

**1. "I understand, because I have been through..."** We think we are empathizing by giving forth our own example of when we experienced the

---

18 From George Carlin's album, Class Clown.
https://www.biography.com/legal-figures/george-carlin-seven-words-supreme-court
https://youtu.be/lqvLTJfYnik?si=YLNTmIW18VuhtR0t

very same thing, but really this is an example of narcissism in conversation, and it's not helpful. When empathizing with a co-worker's plight, or being present for a family member who needs to vent, you need to let the person know that you do, indeed, understand them. Your example or anecdote can come later if you even get that far. "Yes, I know what you mean, when I called his office, he said this to me, blah, blah, blah…" will not help.

2."**Always**" or "**Never**." Avoid using definitive words or get ready for the blowback if you do! There's no wiggle room when you tell someone you are dead set certain that their behavior has always been this way or never that. Being so definite leaves no room for interpretation or growth.

3. "**Well, things happen for a reason.**" "What will be is will be." "It's all for the best." Multitudinous platitudes are a dime-a-dozen, and just as worthless. If you cough them up, you are sending a clear message that you are skirting across the top of the conversation, hoping it's over ASAP. How well could you possibly be listening if respond with these useless phrases?

4. "**Well, what did you learn?**" This response is the provenance of the parent or teacher. Generally speaking, any obstacle we come up against presents a potential learning experience. But do you want to be asked what you learned from a crisis when you're looking for sympathy? Does any adult ever really want to be spoken to like a child? That's a rhetorical question, because the obvious answer is an emphatic no.

5. "**That's just like last time when you…**" "I'm not surprised, I've seen you do this before." Just like when using "always" and "never," reminding your spouse, child, or an employee of their repeated behavior in the face of their bemoaning something that clearly comes from their own behavior, really, will not a friendly conversation make! Most people do not want to be reminded of cause-and-effect, even when they very well may have been the cause. Avoid instructing as best you can; just be sympathetic.

Ultimately what we want with the words we use in an emotionally intelligent way is for people to respond, rather than react. As you can't always know which circumstances might trigger someone, neither can you be sure of every word that will set someone off. However, you can avoid the above five dirty phrases to improve.

Communication is critical in the efficient operation of any business. We are living in an age where words are truncated and symbols and smiley faces take the place of actual responses. We are speaking less than we ever have before, but words still matter. They doubly do when someone comes to you with a crisis, or merely needs to vent for a bit. How you apply emotional intelligence in your reply will determine if that person opts to reach out to you again in the future.

# 28 Conclusion

Allow me to reference a classic line from my favorite movie, *The Godfather*: "This is business, it's not personal."

I do believe all the advice one ever needs can be directly taken from *Godfather* quotes when it comes to emotional intelligence in the dental office. But as much as I hate to go against my favorite film—*business is personal.*

I don't want my life to be any other way. Having discovered emotional intelligence, taken a deep dive to learn, apply, and now teach it to my coaching clients, EI permeates every aspect of my life. From work to play to family relationships, everything for me is indeed personal or informed by my feelings and emotions. And I revel in this fact.

Before I learned about EI, I sensed that we humans don't really do so well when we try to compartmentalize our lives. Yes, you can work hard trying to do so, acting one way in the office with your coworkers, and displaying another side with your kids.

However, I think trying to keep such strictly delineated lines from bleeding over into one another in your life really takes a toll. It's like the serially cheating spouse. The consistent hiding of such a deep secret erodes at one's psyche in ways the cheater might never realize, while the spouse who is cheated on often notices the cracks in the armor of deceit.

Nowhere in this book, however, have I suggested you be an open book to everyone you encounter. Surely you have to consider each situation, and each person, on a case-by-case basis. I'd venture to guess that you do not have the same type of intimacies with coworkers as you do with your family. Your best buddy might be the person you tell your every secret to, but your spouse knows your heart in a way no other person on the planet could ever imagine.

Hiding your emotional intelligence from your coworkers or showering them with caring, yet remaining stoic and unapproachable with your spouse also won't do. Leaving the best part of you with just one group of folks is not natural.

## Being the Best You, While Not Annoying Anybody Else

Ok, so you got through this book. You're ready. You're able. You're willing.

I'm sorry to tell you, though…You're not going to wake up in the next few days and be able to see through walls like a superhero. You are most likely not going to be skipping down the street, hovering over a patient's saliva-dripping maw, or watching late night reruns and be knocked back with a, "Now, it is all so clear to me! I have evolved into an all-knowing, compassionate human, and I will go forth unto the world and bring everyone I come into contact with a wonderful, warm glow."

No, this emotional intelligence stuff sneaks up on you. You can't force it, and you won't suddenly become a new person, able to clearly see the difference between the old you and the new.

Like the old mercury fillings spreading to fill the void in the tooth, EI fills in the cracks to help us become a stronger, better human.

We acclimate as our awareness grows and our world becomes less restrictive. We become more than a smidgen happier. But it is a slow process or growth.

What WILL happen is that you'll suddenly find you're able to give yourself a few seconds to consider your actions before you act. From there, if you don't let old habits come back to bite your keister (which they certainly can) and you don't get too wrapped up in trying to battle back somebody else's less-than-stellar self-awareness, your emotional intelligence will probably grow exponentially.

It's a Pandora's Box kind of a thing. Once out, it doesn't go back in. Like the muscles you come to form and grow the more you play tennis or the brain cells that multiply when use your noggin to learn some deep German philosophy, emotional intelligence becomes pretty much a "you-get-better-the-more-you-use-it" scenario.

Please remember though, all this better-you building doesn't usually come with a round of applause, let alone recognition from others. Most of the time the things that you do, especially when it comes to giving to another, might only rate on your own radar.

Read that again. I pasted it again here:

Please remember though, all this better-you building doesn't usually come with a round of applause, let alone recognition from others. Most of the time the things that you do, especially when it comes to giving to another, might only rate on your own radar.

This doesn't mean you should not go forth and live your emotional intelligence to the maximum. If you do use your emotional intelligence, you make people's lives around you better with the empathy and awareness that you are growing.

It's just that if you are looking for a pat on the back or a passing "thanks," you might not get it.

You will, however, become a better parent, boss, partner, sibling, etc. You'll come to notice that you are the one people come to for solace or advice or just a safe port in a storm. This emotional intelligence stuff consistently makes your life better in the smallest of way. It's just that those ways are not always decipherable at first blush.

Please, step lightly.

Remember, not everybody is aware of or even cares to go through growing their emotional intelligence, and you can't force them. Let's rephrase that and say, the more aware you do become, the more growth you go through, the less you will take it upon yourself to want to change anybody but yourself.

So, really, that last point is one of the big trade secrets here, something you'll undoubtedly come to digest the better you get at this EI stuff: *You can't change anybody other than yourself.*

All the best emotional intelligence in the world won't give you the super-power to be so influential over your fellow humans that you change them.

I wish couples, siblings, bosses, and employees would come to this aware-ness, but so often they don't. How much easier would it be on us all if we all just accepted the fact that we need to first and foremost stay in the confines of our heads and clean up our own house first, before looking at the mess in somebody else's garage?

I have written countless times in this book that we can influence others with a better working EI, and this is true. But real change of the self has to come from the self who wants to change.

Even if you do get recognized for your new awareness, sometimes using emotional intelligence is met with resistance or utter scorn. Whether con-fronting a passive-aggressive neighbor trying to build his fence across your property or shutting down an office kerfuffle as quickly as you can, emotional intelligence will win the day, but sometimes the people you come in contact with don't want it to win.

Even when emotional intelligence prevails, you may get adverse reactions from trying to be the diplomat, bringing warring parties together, or just being nice when all around you aren't being civil. Sometimes coming along with your newly realized EI might indeed break the big logjam, other times, it won't.

Remember schemas and habits? A lot of people don't particularly want these parts of their psyche challenged or even jostled a little bit.

Check your frustration at the door when it comes to how slowly emotional intelligence might be flowing in you and those around you. An oft-repeated phrase by psychologists, and one you may have heard me use before is: "Don't shoulda all over yourself."

## When EI Goes Off Track

I warned you earlier that certain people indeed grow great awareness only to use it to some nefarious ends. Of course, this negative application of EI runs counter to what emotional intelligence teaches us—really, how much EI do you have if you turn around and use it to tweak someone or to roll out your passive-aggressive behavior?

In a Dale Carnegie[19]-like universe where too many men and women are looking to "win friends and influence people," there are people looking to use our feelings, triggers, and needs against us. The upside is that the more emotionally intelligent you are, the more you will be able to catch these folks pretty quickly. And of course, I know that you, as my gentle, wonderful reader, won't be heading down this path.

The other way emotional intelligence can go off the rails slightly is when a person cultivates acutely effective emotional intelligence with others, almost to an empathic degree, but fails to be so acutely aware of themselves. This is a very rare occurrence. Usually EI works like that old, "you can't love somebody unless you love yourself first" platitude. But there are indeed people do well giving to others, sympathizing and continually offering themselves up as the bearer of good advice and the ultimate sounding board, but they don't have a clue as to what their own needs are or what triggers them.

The person who suffers this particular misfire often displays specific symptoms. They will cover their stunted awareness with humor, sickening optimism, or by playing the proverbial doormat. Admittedly, the employees with an optimistic (or doormat) boss might think they have an advantage they can rightly play when it comes to seeking perks or raises. In a family, kids all too readily know which parent is the pushover. Still, there are as many detrimental consequences in being this type of person as there are in dealing with them.

The person with an all-knowing, all-giving disposition will find themselves wrung dry. If everyone comes to you for advice or that shoulder to cry on, you may come to find that nobody is ready, willing, or even aware that you might occasionally need that shoulder for yourself.

We might stop seeking the advice of the overly optimistic cheerleader or a partner who constantly reaches for humor when presented with a problem. I have also seen partners (of all kinds) begin to resent someone who is just too easily manipulated. Undoubtedly, children respond better when certain boundaries are set for them, as do, dare I say, adults.

Lastly, there is a school of thought that weighs in on too many emotional expressions getting in the way of critical thinking. Throughout this book, I have cautioned about throwing away logical reasoning for only your gut feelings. Mind and heart, like action and reaction, must work hand in hand. When real awareness is honed to a fine edge you will know when to balance out the situation or person you are encountering with precisely what's needed for the criteria presented you. This won't come even from a conscious thought on your part. It will all just prove instinctive.

Our critical thinking is in no danger of becoming weaker as we build our emotional intelligence, although this is something critics of EI like to claim. In fact, our thinking becomes stronger when we get everything working in sync: our mind, emotion, knowledge of our needs, and the needs of others. When everything works together, we will see the rewards of it.

---

19 https://www.dalecarnegie.com/en

## Perfection: Forget It!

You need to be ever aware, that even after reading this so informative and entertaining book, digesting all I have to say and applying it in your life, you are still going to come up short. You are a human being. And hate to break this to you though I must, I need remind you.

**You aren't perfect. You can't be.**

You've read about many things that stands in your way, either biologically or emotionally, to building emotional intelligence. Yes, you can battle lots of this stuff and battle it better with more awareness. Still, frailties and weirdness exist in various measure in every one of us, and will be there until the day we die. I believe the best any of us can do is try and live those three quotes that opened this book:

*"The secret to many a man's success in the world resides in his insight into the moods of men and his tact in dealing with them."* ~J.G. HOLLAND[20]

J.G. Holland suggests that the secret to success is in gaining "insight into the moods of men" exacting "tact in dealing with them." This translates as much to trying to know what another is thinking (sensing our fellows' triggers and moods) as to exerting our empathy and maybe a smidgen of our influence on them. Of course, one can't come to this awareness unless one has knowledge of their own emotional state.

*Be the person your dog thinks you are!"* ~J.W. STEPHENS[21]

J.W. Stephens' quote "Be the person your dog thinks you are!" might not seem to be related to emotional intelligence, but think about what your dog feels about you. Dogs generally shower their owners with complete and utter devotion. Our dogs, like no other creature really, think we are the most wonderful person on the planet. All they want to do is cuddle up near us and be present in our presence. If we could only be this wonderful to other humans we meet, to lighten up everybody's day, and to have both coworkers and family just love being around us.

And have you ever noticed how we always reciprocate this affection to our dogs? We seem always happy to see this creature who only ever gives us complete unadulterated love.

How do we cultivate this doggy love and devotion in our fellow humans? Do I need to tell you how spreading healthy doses of emotional intelligence around engenders warm feelings? You might not get the obligatory slobbery lick on the cheek, but you might get people who are damn glad to see you every time you walk in the door.

20 https://www.masslive.com/springfield/2019/07/josiah-gilbert-holland-recalling-famed-newspaper-columnist-on-200th-anniversary-of-his-birth.html
21 https://a.co/d/68uzqEX

*"The most important thing in life is to always be yourself. Unless you can be Batman, in which case, always be Batman."* ~UNKNOWN

The last quote I admit was me being slightly silly, as much to get your attention when you flipped open the front cover as to make a subtle point: "The most important thing in life is always to be yourself. Unless you can be Batman, in which case, always be Batman." This means that first and foremost you should always be yourself, but if that's beyond your reach (which it isn't), then it might not be so bad being somebody like Batman. He's trustworthy, a defender of the weak, and a multibillionaire with a cool cave and a bunch of incredible crime-fighting toys.

You get the point I am trying to make here, right? There are just some qualities we need to cultivate that make us better bosses, partners, siblings, and employees. These qualities are all fed and nurtured by a greater emotional intelligence.

## Go Forth and Do

Theories are all well and good, and God knows I do like to hear myself type.

But in the end, nothing I've given you here is worth anything unless you go out and apply it in the real world. Along the way, I've dropped little bons mots of how to find, build and approach your awareness, like how to face a passive-aggressor, and how to have a more substantive sit down with your spouse. I've played out a few real-life examples that I've come across at my practices to illustrate what you could come up against. I have even let you in on a smidgen of the craziness that I go through in the ever-constant swirl that is my thought processes. These are things we all have to deal with in one way or another on a daily basis. I've also cautioned you about the enemies of emotional intelligence. But really, if you don't go forth and live this book, well, all the talk will be just that…talk.

As much as emotional intelligence cannot thrive in a vacuum, that compartmentalizing I mentioned at the start of this chapter, it also doesn't work if it is ever only used as lip service. Salovey and Mayer, Dr. Daniel Goleman, and all the other men and women who have explored and consistently work on the nuts and bolts of what EI is, prompt readers and symposium audiences to go out and do. Live emotional intelligence, grow awareness to apply it, and attempt to empathize at all times. Learn as much as you can about why you do what you do, so you can come to understand why others do what they do.

Really, we are all sitting around a little too much these days anyway. Take a walk through the office and listen to what your staff is going on about, and sit across from your kid and have a conversation. Take a friend out for coffee and see what's going on in their lives. Get your hands dirty, in a figurative sense. (Or literal if you like to garden.) You've read this book, now go and use that emotional intelligence.

It's time I leave you, my dear gentle reader, now completely evolved and aware. I can't thank you enough for taking this ride with me. Please feel free to drop me a line anytime you like (write me here: drsteve@thedentistwhogetsit. com) and tell me of your personal challenges with emotional intelligence.

Shoot me a story or two of what you've come up against, offer up any solutions that I didn't get into in my chapters. We all know enough by now that one of the essential things emotional intelligence teaches us is to always be on the lookout for new approaches, and to consider somebody else's insights. in a word, to listen. I am listening, and I certainly do want to hear from you.

I hope for your ever-more emotionally intelligent days ahead, and for your practices, as well as for your lives, to continue to grow healthy and prosperous. Now get out and make your life, and those of the people you care about, better.

~Dr. Steven Hymovitch

www.ingramcontent.com/pod-product-compliance
Lightning Source LLC
Chambersburg PA
CBHW052116030426
42335CB00025B/3016